ENJOY

ENJOY

ALAN BENNETT

FABER AND FABER

LONDON   BOSTON

First published in 1980
by Faber and Faber Limited
3 Queen Square London WC1N 3AU
Printed in Great Britain by
Latimer Trend & Company Ltd Plymouth
All rights reserved

British Library Cataloguing in Publication Data

Bennett, Alan, *b. 1934*
Enjoy.
I. Title
822'.9'14   PR 60 52.ESE/

ISBN 0-571-11734-1

Characters

WILFRED CRAVEN (DAD)
CONNIE CRAVEN (MAM)
MS CRAIG
LINDA CRAVEN
HERITAGE
ANTHONY
GREGORY
MRS CLEGG
ADRIAN
SID
HARMAN
CHARLES
ROWLAND

Enjoy was first presented on 15 October 1980, at the Vaudeville Theatre, by Michael Codron with the following cast:

WILFRED CRAVEN	Colin Blakely
CONNIE CRAVEN	Joan Plowright
MS CRAIG	Philip Sayer
LINDA CRAVEN	Susan Littler
HERITAGE	Roger Alborough
ANTHONY	Julian Ronnie
GREGORY	Stephen Flynn
MRS CLEGG	Joan Hickson
ADRIAN	Graham Wyles
SID	Michael Hughes
HARMAN	Marc Sinden
CHARLES	Simon Painter
ROWLAND	Gareth Price

Directed by Ronald Eyre

Author's Note

Playgoers who find that this text does not coincide with what they heard in the theatre may assume that the cast just did not know their lines. They will (I hope) be wrong. The text here printed is that of the play prior to rehearsal and production. In the past my plays have always altered (and generally improved) in rehearsal. I imagine this play will do the same. However, I am told that there is some advantage in having a text available to coincide with first production, if only for those members of the first night audience who are unable to believe their ears. So here it is.

ACT ONE

The chorus 'For unto us a child is born' from Handel's Messiah. *The music is cut off sharply in full flow, there is a brief silence and the curtain rises on the living-room of a back-to-back house in the North. The outside door opens directly on to the street and other doors lead to the scullery and the upstairs. It is neat and ordinary and some effort has been made to improve the place. There should be something not quite right about the room . . . Is it that the furniture is too far apart (as it is, for example, in opera)? Or is it islanded in the centre of the stage with space round it . . . a stage upon a stage? Perhaps it's just that the room is too real.*

MAM *and* DAD *are a couple in their sixties. They are discovered in the middle of their marriage.*

DAD *sits in the easy chair by the fire.* MAM *stands.*

DAD: (*Answering a question, with controlled anger*) Sweden.

MAM: Sweden?

DAD: Sweden.

> (MAM *goes into the scullery and* DAD *roots in the depths of the chair for a magazine, which he holds close to his face as his eyes are bad.*
>
> MAM *starts singing 'Fly Home Little Heart' (Novello, King's Rhapsody). She sings well and knows all the words. She stops singing, abruptly, comes back, whereupon* DAD *puts the magazine away.*)

MAM: This room's upside down. (*Pause*) Where? Dad.

DAD: Sweden.

MAM: Sweden. It's news to me is that. (*Pause*) What if anybody comes?

DAD: Feel my arm.

MAM: It's like a tip.

DAD: Two minutes.

9

MAM: It's where they commit suicide and the king rides a
    bicycle, Sweden.

DAD: Mam.

MAM: I don't want to feel your arm. What do I want to feel your
    arm for? I'm always feeling your arm. Feel your own arm.
    (*She feels his arm.*) You use this arm, you.

DAD: That's the point: I don't use it. I can't use it. I can't feel
    it.

MAM: It's an excuse. You curry sympathy. Do you feel that?
    (DAD *shakes his head.*)
    This?
    (DAD *shakes his head again.*)

DAD: Don't stop.

MAM: I'm bored.

DAD: You've nothing better to do.

MAM: I have. I've the milk bottles to put out.
    (MAM *goes back into the scullery.*)

DAD: It wants a different environment. The new flats have this
    underfloor central heating.

MAM: (*Off*) You've let it beat you, that arm. You want to make it
    a challenge, something to be overcome. That's today's
    philosophy with handicaps. You see it on TV all the time.
    There's people with far worse than your arm gone on to not
    bad careers.

DAD: I've no feeling in one arm; I've got a steel plate in my
    head; I can hardly see and you talk about a career. I thought
    I was retired.

MAM: (*Off*) I wish women could retire. (*Pause*) What have I
    come in here for?

DAD: I haven't lost my gift for responsibility. That's something
    you never lose, the ability to command respect. Milk bottles.
    I had six men under me.

MAM: (*Returning with the bottles*) Well it's not a bad little biscuit
    barrel. Women don't get biscuit barrels choose how long
    they work.

DAD: Once we get shifted I plan to take an active part in the
    community association; I was thinking in bed last night I
    might take up French.

MAM: As the victim of a hit-and-run driver I think you're entitled to put your feet up. (*She is at the door putting the milk bottles out.*) Smoke rising from the Grasmeres. The toll of destruction goes on. I've no tears left. (*She sits down again.*) Where did you say Linda's gone?
(DAD *groans.*)
I felt your arm.

DAD: Sweden. Sweden. Linda has gone to Sweden.

MAM: I won't ask you again.

DAD: You will.

MAM: I won't. I'll think about something else. (*Pause*) My mother lost her memory. I think.
(*Pause*)
(*Looking at a magazine.*) They're bonny curtains. Only they're nylon. I wouldn't have nylon. Smells, nylon. I wouldn't have any man-made fibres. Wool, cotton, you can't go wrong.
'Try these easy to make prepared in advance menus and be a relaxed and carefree hostess when the doorbell rings.'
(*Pause*)
Have I asked you where Linda has gone?

DAD: Yes.

MAM And have you told me?

DAD: Yes.

MAM: I know then? (*She looks miserable.*)

DAD: Sweden, Sweden, Sweden, Sweden. Sweden.
(*Pause*)

MAM: We're under siege here. Pulling down good property. It's a sin.

DAD: I think of the future.

MAM: When I was a girl there were droves and droves of houses like these. You'd see them from the railway, streets of them, the stock of every town and city in the country. What's become of the old estates? Streets were played in when we were little, courted in when we were young . . . Harringtons, Hawkesworths, Gilpins, Grasmeres . . . groves deserted, drives emptied, terraces reaped of every house. Rubble.

DAD: Light! Air!

MAM: We're a relic. An ancient monument. We are living in the last back-to-backs in Leeds. (*She goes into the scullery singing 'Bless This House' (Brahe).*)

DAD: I have high hopes of the maisonette, Mam. I mean it to be a new start. A different going on.

(MAM *sings on.*)

I'm looking forward to the chrome-plated handles on the bath. That'll transform my life. And non-slip vinyl. Vinyl throughout. There's even vinyl in the lifts.

MAM: (*Returning*) It's best not to expect too much. The worst is the most I intend to expect. Then I shan't be disappointed.

DAD: No more trailing to the bin. Just chuck it down the chute. It's the last word in waste disposal.

MAM: They pee in those lifts. It takes more than a bit of vinyl to alter human nature.

DAD: It's south facing so I was thinking in bed last night I can go in for a few tomatoes.

MAM: They found a baby down one of those chutes.

DAD: We could be self-sufficient where tomatoes are concerned. I shall sit out on that bit of grass.

MAM: Another mecca for dogs.

DAD: It's a new life beginning! (*He opens his arms wide in an expansive gesture.*) Come, bulldozer, come!

MAM: What's she doing going to Sweden? I bumped into her in the scullery last night and I don't remember anything about Sweden. She didn't look like someone going to Sweden. I wonder where she does go sometimes.

DAD: She's a personal secretary. She goes where she's told. That's the nature of her employment.

MAM: She's just this minute come back from some other place abroad. West Germany was it? Now it's Sweden.

DAD: That's the contemporary world.

MAM: She didn't have any luggage. You have luggage if you're going to Sweden.

DAD: Not in this day and age. It's like popping across the road. A new world. And don't go calling our Linda.

MAM: I'm not calling her. I'm only saying you don't waltz out of the house empty-handed last thing at night saying, 'I'm going to Sweden', even if it is the twentieth century.

DAD: What do you know about the twentieth century? I know one thing. She'd feel my arm. She loves me does Linda.

MAM: If we're talking of love I know somebody else who'd have liked Sweden, somebody else with whom it'd 've struck a chord.

DAD: Guide-books, street-plans: she'll have Stockholm at her fingertips.

MAM: I admit the person in question generally made a bee-line for the Mediterranean, but given the right circumstances he wouldn't have said No to Scandinavia. Talking of love.

DAD: If I know her boss it'll be one long round of conferences, our Linda there at his elbow. Still she'll generally manage to snatch an hour or two from her gruelling schedule to take in the principal sights. She might even get to a sauna. It's where saunas originated, Sweden.

MAM: They've spread to Leeds now, talking of love.

DAD: Sweden boasts some fine modern architecture plus a free-wheeling attitude towards personal morality. But our Linda's a sensible girl: she won't be bowled over by that.

MAM: He always had a level head. Only he was quite happy to stay at home. He was the stay-at-home type. Talking of love.

DAD: Then why didn't he?

MAM: Why didn't he what?

DAD: Stop at home.

(*Pause*)

MAM: Dad.

DAD: What?

MAM: How will anybody find us when we move?

DAD: Who?

MAM: Anybody anxious to locate us. With the house pulled down where will they start?

DAD: Who?

MAM: A casual visitor, say. A one-off caller. Anybody.

DAD: You send out cards. They give you cards to send out.

MAM: That's nice.

(*Pause*)

Dad. What if it's someone you can't send a card to because

13

you've lost touch?

DAD: Too bad.

MAM: The Corporation's bound to keep a schedule. You'll be able to walk into the Town Hall and find out where we've been put. They'll keep track—we pay rates.

DAD: It won't happen. He'll not come.

MAM: Who?

DAD: I won't say his name.

MAM: How do I know to whom you're referring then? Who, Dad?

DAD: You won't get his name out of me.

MAM: I wonder if he's famous: he went to London.

DAD: Yes, we know what for.

MAM: Its institutions and libraries. Its public buildings, the concerts, art galleries and places of interest.

DAD: Not forgetting its superb toilet facilities. The dimly lit charms of its public conveniences. Purlieus of that nature. Talking of love.

(*Silence*)

MAM: Sweden was where Mr and Mrs Broadbent went last year. One of these winter-break things. Very reasonable apparently: they couldn't get over the public transport.

DAD: You want to forget about him.

MAM: Who?

DAD: You're losing your memory, capitalize on it and forget him. Because I do not want his name mentioned. You will never see him again. He is dead. He does not exist.

MAM: Why am I sitting on this chair? I never sit on this chair. I don't remember ever sitting on this chair before.

(*A knock on the door.*) That must be Linda. She can't have gone to Sweden. She must just have forgotten her key.

(MAM *looks out of the window.*)

It's not Linda. It's a young woman.

DAD: What sort of young woman?

MAM: A young woman. She looks like a total stranger.

DAD: They tell you not to open the door. They put out leaflets.

MAM: Professional type. Little grey costume—blondeish.

DAD: There's all sorts now. The women are worse than the men.

14

They're devoid of conscience. She'll go away.

(*A loud knock.*)

MAM: Very slim. Looks as if she keeps off the carbohydrates.

DAD: Be still.

(*They wait.*

Another knock.

DAD *gets up. Looks. Goes to the door. Shouts through the letter-box.*)

DAD: Listen. We're on the telephone and there's an Alsatian within earshot. So get lost.

(DAD *is coming away from the door when there is another knock.*)

Be told. You have come to the wrong house.

MAM: She may be from the Corporation, it's a smart little costume. (*Shouting through the letter-box.*) If it's about the new flat we're waiting to be allocated; we're an oldish couple; we don't have that many visitors.

(*A piece of paper is put through the letter-box.*

They let it lie for a moment, looking at it, then MAM *picks it up.*)

(*Reading*) 'This neighbourhood is shortly to be demolished.' Well, we know that. 'In the past, redevelopment has often ignored many valuable elements in the social structure of traditional communities such as this. Their sense of identity has been lost and with it the virtues of self-reliance, neighbourliness and self-help.' This is going to take some studying out. 'Your council is anxious to avoid the mistakes of the past and preserve those qualities.' What qualities? Oh, self-reliance, neighbourliness and self-help. 'It is therefore undertaking a social study of selected families in this area . . .' They do this sort of thing now. It's the sort of thing they do. 'This card will be shown to you by a qualified sociologist. Kindly admit him/her to your home as an observer. The observer will not speak.' (Oh.) 'Try not to engage him/her in conversation as this may falsify the true picture of your home life he/she needs if this project is to succeed. The name of your observer is Ms Craig. Your co-operation is appreciated. R. S. Harman. Projects Director.' I've seen his picture in the *Evening Post*, cutting a ribbon.

DAD: No.

MAM: We must have been selected; they've picked us out down at the Town Hall.

DAD: It's an intruder.

MAM: They couldn't go to twenty-six with him being black: they'll know we're a bit more classy. Fasten your trousers. (*Through the letter-box.*) We shan't keep you a moment. (*She tidies the already tidy room.*)

DAD: It's been on the wireless: don't open your door.

MAM: She's only going to observe us. They put a premium on consultation nowadays. We ought to be flattered. And she's a striking woman. Of course, it's a goodish salary now, local government.

DAD: She's come to kill me.

MAM: She's not above twenty-five.

DAD: She'll kill me.

MAM: Kill you? She's got one of these new briefcases, I've seen them in Schofields. She's from the Council. They don't kill you from the Council: what with social workers, meals on wheels and one thing and another all their efforts are the other way. They want to keep you alive. Come to kill you! Take one of your tablets.

DAD: There'll be murder.

(*Another knock.*)

I'm telling you. Don't open it.

MAM: Don't. Don't. It's always don't. The doors I could have opened if it hadn't been for you. My voice would have opened any door. I could have been in the Choral Society, sung on the stage of the Victoria Hall. I could have been rubbing shoulders with doctors' wives, solicitors, people with their own transport. I could have been going out to coffee mornings in select neighbourhoods, mixing with all sorts. I could have blossomed half a dozen times over. But no. Why? You. You, Dad, you.

DAD: Connie.

(DAD *rises from the chair.* MAM *pushes him back.*)

MAM: Sit down. We'll see if she kills you. Coming.

(*She unlocks the door.*

*There is a slight pause, long enough for one to begin to wonder
if there is still anybody there, then the door is pushed smartly
back and to the strains of 'Waltz of My Heart' (Novello,* The
Dancing Years) MS CRAIG *comes in, walks straight across the
room with no hesitation at all, sits on an upright chair down
stage, puts down her handbag at one side of the chair, takes out
a pad and waits, pen in hand.*

MS CRAIG *is a man. Not a man in outrageous drag, a man who
is a woman perhaps but nevertheless a man.*

Silence.

MAM *looks at him/her for a long time.*

DAD *keeps looking and looking away. He can't see* MS CRAIG *all
that clearly.*)

MAM: How do you do. Pleased to meet you.

(MS CRAIG *looks coolly at them with no response whatsoever.*)
This is my husband, Mr Craven. And I'm Mrs Craven.
We're The Cravens.

(*Pause*)

DAD: I'm frightened, Mam.

MAM: Then have one of your tablets. He gets over-anxious. It's
not mental. He's the victim of a hit-and-run driver. Don't
start yet, this isn't typical yet. I'm sorry the place is upside
down, I haven't had a chance to get round this morning,
that's not typical either. Haven't we been having some
weather?

DAD: Mam!

MAM: She's starting.

DAD: Connie.

MAM: Shut up.

(*Silence.*)

Our visitor hasn't picked the most comfortable chair, has she,
Dad? (*Pause*) Though I've read that a straight back is better
for you. (*Pause*) Bad backs seem to be on the increase.
(*Pause*) It must be to do with sitting habits. One way and
another. (*Desperately*) My sister-in-law had a terrible back
and they put that down to lolling about in easy chairs, only
then it turned out that she had a progressive disease of the
spine. Which she died of. Unfortunately. (*Pause*)

17

DAD: It was a slipped disc.

MAM: It wasn't a slipped disc. It was a long-term illness.

DAD: How do you know? You can't remember.

(MS CRAIG *makes a note.*)

Mam. She's just made a note. What did I say?

(MS CRAIG *writes something else down.*)

Look, Mam.

MAM: I'm taking no notice. (*Whispering*) Dad, what is the survey about again?

(DAD *hands her the schedule and* MAM *reads it again.*)

I have a tendency to forget: one of the penalties of getting older. I take after my mother; she suffered with her memory. Is it to do with us being happy? Is that the gist of it? We are.

DAD: And if we're not, we shouldn't let on to you.

MAM: We are anyway, by and large. Put down happy. Not discontented.

DAD: We will be happy once we're out of this midden.

MAM: It used to be one of the better streets, this. You were always thought to be a bit more refined if you lived in this street. It was that bit classier. None of them are very classy now.

DAD: Course they're not classy. How can they be classy when they're flattened?

MAM: Mr Craven's always been on the side of progress: he had false teeth when he was twenty-seven. Notice too that this is an end house, giving us three downstairs windows as opposed to two in the other houses. I don't know whether that's relevant.

DAD: I had six men under me.

MAM: We've been very happy all in all. I'd offer you a cup of tea but if we're meant to behave as if you're not here I can't, can I?

(MS CRAIG *writes something down.*)

Don't put me on record as not having offered though. If you were an ordinary run-of-the-mill visitor I would.

DAD: We never have any visitors.

MAM: Only because we're not well served by public transport.

I'd like to have gone in for these coffee mornings. You read about them in magazines: functions in the home in aid of one thing and another. Like-minded people. Only Mr Craven's not keen on company. One of the big might-have-beens. I'll make some tea. You go on behaving normally, Dad.

(MAM *goes into the scullery singing 'I Can Give You the Starlight' (Novello,* The Dancing Years). *She calls from the scullery.*)

We're waiting for our Linda. (*Pause*) We think she may have gone somewhere. (*Pause*) Where is it we think she's gone, Dad?

DAD: *Sweden.*

MAM: Mr Craven worships Linda. (*Pause*) Tell her about Linda, Dad.

DAD: Shut up about Linda.

(MS CRAIG *writes something down.*)

She's a personal secretary.

MAM: She's a personal secretary. She's our only daughter.

DAD: Our only child. Goes all over. Last week it was West Germany. You've never been to West Germany, I bet. She spent Christmas in the Lebanon. A grand girl. Everything a father could wish for.

(MAM *returns.*)

MAM: She's quite at home in hotels; can choose from a menu without turning a hair. He's deeply proud of her. Where is it she's gone?

DAD: I said to her last time she was home: Did you ever dream you'd be in Beirut? But she's very modest: she just laughed.

MAM: Just laughed. Where was it she liked? Antwerp, was it?

DAD: Antwerp! *Hamburg.*

MAM: I forget, you see. My mother was like that. It's boys that generally travel. Daughters are more the stay-at-home type. Linda's different.

DAD: She was a wanderer, right from being a kiddy. It was always: Get out the atlas, Dad. Let me sit on your knee. Show me Las Vegas, Dad. Rio de Janeiro.

MAM: Sat on his knee. Las Vegas. Rio de Janeiro.

DAD: They advertised for a Girl Friday. Someone with the ability to arrange small private lunches and take creative decisions in a crisis. She's strong on both those points.

MAM: She takes air travel in her stride. It's a shame she's not here. You'd have had something in common.

DAD: What?

MAM: Both career women.

DAD: There's no comparison.

MAM: He idolizes Linda. Only she's not normal for girls round here.

DAD: Normal? She's exceptional. You won't find girls like Linda stood on every street corner. Girls with no advantages who are in a position to fly off to Scandinavia at five minutes' notice.

MAM: They've both done well.

(*At 'both'* MS CRAIG *looks up.*)

DAD: I can hear a kettle.

MAM: Right from the start we were determined neither of them should have to go through what we went through.

DAD: I can hear a kettle. Make the bloody tea, go on.

(DAD *makes some threatening move towards* MAM *with his stick as she goes.*)

Go with her. Go on.

(MS CRAIG *doesn't stir.*)

So it's me you're watching? Not her. What for? There's only me, sitting. (*Pause*) And that's not real, not accurate. Because you're here too. You spoil it. Go away and I might be natural. Me alone in a room. What's that like? You'll never know. Private, madam. My secret. (*Pause*) And don't think you're going to pick up any information about me and her either. Our so-called sexual relations. If that's the sort of gen you're after you go out of here on your arse. I make no apology for using that word. On your arse. I know you want to know. You're just the sort of casual caller that does. Well, no. No. No. (*He bangs his stick closer to her but she does not flinch.*) Write *that* down. (*She doesn't. Pause*) Still, I'm not an unreasonable man. You've got your job to do. And I don't want to give you the idea I'm trying to hide something, or that anything unorthodox goes on between my wife and me. It doesn't. Nothing goes on. Nothing at all. I don't know whether that's unorthodox. Judging from all these magazines it probably is. No foreplay. No afterplay. And fuck all in between. But don't expect me to expand on that. What made you do this job?

(MS CRAIG *makes a note.*)

So far as the formal sex act is concerned, in the actual performance of sexual intercourse, or coitus or whatever you were brought up to say, I start off at some disadvantage. I've no feeling in this arm and I can hardly see. Which knocks out at least three erogenous zones for a kick-off. I was run over down at Four Lane Ends.

(*In the scullery* MAM *is singing 'We'll Gather Lilacs' (Novello,* Perchance to Dream).)

I was on a crossing. I was within my rights. He came straight at me. It wasn't a genuine accident. I don't think it was an accident at all. It was a deliberate attempt at murder. The police kept the file open for months but they never found him. Do you drive? I expect so. They all have cars on the Council. I don't bear a grudge. I did bear a grudge for a long time, only now they've put me on tablets, since when the grudge has gone. But there's no feeling in that arm. I couldn't tell if this hand was wet or dry, if you understand me. It's numb. Grip it. Go on. Grip it hard. Listen, I'm old enough to be your father. You can't afford to turn your nose up at me. Bite it. Go on. Bite the bugger.

(*She doesn't.*)

No, you're like her. You're two of a kind. She won't either.

MAM: (*From scullery*) How do you like your tea, Dad?

DAD: We've been married twenty-five years. Strong. I like it strong. 'Dad.' You never asked me my name. It's Wilfred. Wilf. Only it never gets used. Always Dad. It's practically new, my name; it's hardly been used since we were first married. It's kept for best. She'll use it when I'm dying, you'll see. She'll fetch it out then.

(*Pause*)

Linda touches it. Linda strokes it. Linda wants the feeling

back. She's a saint is Linda. Only what good's that when she's in bloody Sweden?

(MAM *comes in with a nice tea-tray*.)

MAM: Who are you talking to?

DAD: I'm talking to madam.

MAM: There's nobody here, Dad. Nobody here at all. (*She winks at* MS CRAIG.) We're just having a normal day.

DAD: Where's my beaker? Which cups are these? We don't use these cups.

MAM: (*Sotto voce*) Dad.

(DAD *belches*.)

Pardon.

DAD: What?

MAM: Beg pardon. I don't know what sort of impression this young lady's getting. I'm trying to behave normally and you seem bent on showing us up.

(DAD *gets up*.)

Where are you going?

DAD: For a piss.

(MRS CRAVEN *is mortified*.)

MAM: He wouldn't say that normally. He'd say anything but that. Pay a visit. Spend a penny. There's half a dozen ways you can get round it if you make the effort. He's just trying to impress.

DAD: Well what about you?

MAM: What?

DAD: Normally every time I get up to go to the lav, you say 'Don't wet on the floor.'

MAM: I never do.

DAD: Without fail. She does 'Don't wet on the floor, Dad.' (*He goes*.)

MAM: I don't say that. I promise. Though he is very slapdash. He puts it down to his arm but frankly I think he doesn't concentrate.

(*Pause*)

We were the first couple in this street to install an inside toilet. You could say we were pioneers in that department. Then everybody else followed suit. (*Pause*) When we first came there was all that having to go down the street. I never liked that. (*Pause*) Mr Craven's not been well. He's on tablets. The aftermath of being run over. One of these hit-and-run drivers. Are you motorized? Practically everybody is nowadays. Without a car you're static. It was after his accident he started imagining things. Someone was trying to kill him. Dr Sillitoe's got him on tablets for depression. It's not mental, in fact it's quite widespread. A lot of better-class people get it apparently. I'm surprised I haven't had it because you're more at risk if you're sensitive, which I am. More than Dad anyway. Only it's not mental. Health is a great gift. He reckons he'll be better once we get into these horrible new flats but I have my doubts. They're not the high flats. Not the multis. They've discontinued those. It's a maisonette. They're built more on the human scale. That's the latest thing now, the human scale. Still I've no need to tell you that, if you're from the Housing.

(DAD *returns.*)

DAD: She's not from the Housing. She's doing a survey. She's seeing how we live. I put her in the picture *vis-à-vis* our sex-lives.

MAM: I think I'll just have a run round with the Ewbank.

DAD: I was telling her in graphic detail how nothing happens.

MAM: I wage a constant battle against dust.

DAD: I was hoping she'd be able to furnish me with some comparative statistics.

MAM: It's having an audience. Saying stuff. Ordinarily speaking we never have a wrong word.

DAD: We do.

MAM: We don't.

DAD: We fucking well do.

MAM: And he doesn't swear.

DAD: I do. I fucking do.

MAM: He doesn't use that word.

DAD: What word?

MAM: The word he just used.

DAD: Well say it. Say it.

23

MAM: NO. That isn't my husband. I forget your name. What is it you're from?

DAD: Read it. Read it. *Read it.* (*He hands* MAM *the paper.*) I'm telling her the same thing sixteen times over.

MAM: You'd better go.

DAD: Sit still.

MAM: You've changed your tune. You didn't want her in here. She was going to kill you. He's all over you now.

DAD: It's something fresh for me, having a witness. It's a change from suffering in silence.

MAM: It's all a performance. For your benefit. We don't live like this. Granted we have the occasional difference but when it's just the two of us we get on like a house on fire.

DAD: It's a hell-hole. I had six men under me.

MAM: He sits there. Never does a hand's turn. Always under my feet. I'm following him round picking up this, wiping up that. Retirement. Women don't retire, do they? When's our whip-round? I keep that toilet like a palace.

DAD: This is her number-one topic. Have you noticed? Have you got that written down? My wife is the world authority on toilets. She has an encyclopaedic knowledge. She could go on TV. One of these general-knowledge programmes, except where normal folks say they know about Wordsworth or Icelandic sagas, she'd opt for toilets.

MAM: Shut up. Don't listen.

DAD: Day in day out, you talk about nothing else.

MAM: I don't. I talk about all sorts. What were we talking about before she knocked at the door? Something. He has me this way, you see, because I can't remember. My memory's poor. My mother was the same. But we have proper conversations. It isn't just toilets. We really run the gamut sometimes. What were we talking about before?

DAD: We were talking about the new flats.

MAM: That's right. Well that's not toilets.

DAD: The chrome handles on the baths.

MAM: You see.

DAD: The vinyl flooring.

MAM: Vinyl flooring. That's right. We were talking about vinyl flooring. We were having a really good conversation about vinyl flooring.

DAD: The flats have vinyl flooring. Vinyl flooring throughout.

MAM: That's right.

DAD: Even in the lifts.

MAM: Yes. (*Absently*) They pee in those lifts.

(MAM *cries out in dismay and covers her face in her hands.* DAD *says nothing but stretches out his arms as if to say 'My wife.'*)

I forget.

DAD: It's not simply you forget. You forget that you do forget half the time. That's what I can't stand. If you could only remember that you forget it'd make it easier. For me.

MAM: Well I do forget. I know that.

DAD: And everything you've said, you've said before. Sixteen times. Every question you ask, you've asked before. Every remark you make, I've heard. I've heard it nineteen times over. Day after day after day.

MAM: We're married.

(*Long pause.*)

There's a couple down the street would do better than us. He's black but she always passes the time of day. They're more typical than we are.

DAD: Stay there.

MAM: If you wanted to go two doors down there's one of these single-parent families. And he's a problem child. That's quite typical of round here too. We're not typical.

DAD: We're not typical because of you. I'm the typical one.

MAM: You're depressed. You're on tablets. That's not typical. There's none of that on our side of the family.

DAD: I may be depressed, only I've still got hopes. This house depresses me. You say I don't help, I've given up trying. Because when I do it's 'Don't use that bucket, that's the outside bucket.' 'Don't use that cloth, I use that to do under the sink.' It's a minefield this house. She's got it all mapped out. The dirty bits and the clean bits. Bits you have to wash your hands after, bits you wash your hands before. And aught that comes into contact with me is dirty. I dirty it.

MAM: Well you do. You don't take care.

DAD: I pollute my own house. Me, I'm the shit on the doorstep.

MAM: That's a word he's heard other people say. He only says it to impress you. It's no crime, cleanliness.

DAD: I am clean.

MAM: You're not. They aren't clean, men. Except our Linda's the same.

DAD: Yes. She's like me is Linda. She's got her priorities right.

MAM: Linda. It's all Linda. Well I had somebody like me, once. He was clean.

DAD: Be quiet.

MAM: Sixteen. Clean. Quiet. Shy.

DAD: Shut up.

MAM: Your own son.

DAD: I haven't got a son.

MAM: You haven't got a son? Who is it I've got in my mind's eye then? A son. A clever son. A son who came top all through school. A lovely, lovely son.

DAD: Gone. Dead. No son.

MAM: No son, no son: no time for son, no room for son. All Linda.

DAD: Shut up about Linda. I love Linda. I love her.

MAM: Yes. I know you do.

(DAD *hits her.*

As he does so, MS CRAIG *involuntarily gets up. It is a startling departure, more startling than the blow, and it has the effect of stopping them dead in their tracks. They both focus on her.*
MS CRAIG *instantly recovers her composure, sits down again and makes a very small note.*
Pause)

MAM: She's written it down, that blow. It'll go on record down at the Town Hall. Next thing is we'll be pestered with social workers.

DAD: I didn't mean it, Connie.

MAM: They won't know that. They'll think that's the normal pattern of events. We should have sent her away.

DAD: We should never have let her in in the first place. We're too old for this guinea-pig lark.

MAM: He never hits me. He's not struck me in ten years!

26

DAD: It eggs you on, somebody sat there. It's all right her saying nothing but that eggs you on more. She wormed all sorts out of me while you were in the scullery, just sitting there.

MAM: Me and all.

DAD: We're in the computer now. Push a button and up will come the particulars. We can forgive and forget but not the computer.

MAM: What have we to be ashamed of? This is a happy marriage.

DAD: I'm turning her out.

MAM: We've done nothing but fratch ever since you arrived. We go for days and never have a wrong word. You aggravate matters, you distort things, watching, sitting there.

DAD: Having to pretend you're not here. You are here, taking it all in. So out, madam. Now. Come on. This is my house. It's my right.

(MS CRAIG *doesn't move*.)

MAM: Go on, love. If Dad thinks it's best you go. (*No response.*) For our sakes! You know what he's like. Dad knows best. It's not just him. We'd both like you to go. We've talked it over.

DAD: Not like. No like about it. I've told you. Get out. And take your notebook with you. (*He picks up* MS CRAIG's *handbag and hands it to her*.) We're fed up of being scrutinized. Condescended to. Criticized implicitly. We don't want somebody educated in this house. So off. Out.

MAM: Don't hit her, Dad. Not her head, Dad.

DAD: Looked at, made notes on. Sized up, pinned down. Assessed, cheapened, dismissed, ridiculed. Well it's over. Finished. Now. Right?

(MS CRAIG *slowly and deliberately rises, when the door opens suddenly and* LINDA *hops in, holding her ankle*.)

LINDA: Shit!

MAM: (*Brightly*) Hello, Linda!

LINDA: *Shit!*

MAM: We thought you'd gone somewhere abroad. Where was it we thought she'd gone, Dad? Somewhere.

LINDA: Shit shit shit.

MAM: Linda's a personal secretary.

(LINDA *isn't a personal secretary.* LINDA *is quite plainly a tart.*)

LINDA: Forty-five quid. Forty-five flaming quid. And the heel's snapped clean off.

MAM: You don't get the workmanship now. Everything's the same. Particularly electrical goods.

LINDA: Listen. These shoes cost nearly fifty quid. They were hand-stitched. Made in Rumania. You can't get better workmanship than that. They're Rumanian pigskin. Only they were designed for use on fitted carpets. Not obstacle courses. Not mountaineering. Have you been outside that door? It's a wilderness!

DAD: Come see your old Dad, Linda. Come give your Dad a kiss and tell us about Scandinavia.

LINDA: Shit.

DAD: Feel my arm.

LINDA: And who are we then? One silk-stockinged leg flung carelessly over the other?

MAM: She's a fellow businesswoman, Linda. It's a survey of some description. Happiness, friendship. It's all official.

DAD: Official trouble.

(LINDA *reads the form.*)

LINDA: Nice costume.

MAM: Linda always had taste. A dress sense came very early.

LINDA: What does 'traditional communities' mean?

MAM: The streets. These houses. Gilpins, Grasmeres, our overall environment.

DAD: The slums.

MAM: We were thinking you'd gone abroad somewhere.

DAD: Sweden.

LINDA: And neighbourliness means that cow next door?

MAM: Mrs Clegg has her good side, Linda. When Dad had shingles she was worth her weight in gold.

LINDA: Sweden? Swindon.

DAD: I had visions of Scandinavia. Swindon's Wiltshire.

LINDA: You just sit here? Is that all she does?

DAD: Yes, and we don't want it. On your way, you. Our Linda comes home to unwind. She's enough on her plate without

you sat there annotating. What was the weather like in
Swindon, love? Have it nice, did you?

LINDA: Stay if you want, sweeheart. I never object to onlookers,
once in a while. It takes all sorts, that's my motto.

MAM: I agree.

LINDA: Brings out the actress in me, if you see what I mean.
Course it's all acting really, isn't it?

DAD: She's wonderful, this girl. Got her philosophy of life
worked out down to the last detail.

MAM: They might find they've got things in common. They've
both got bags of poise.

DAD: Her legs aren't a patch on Linda's.

LINDA: I'm not staying long. It's only a flying visit.

DAD: Foreign parts again, is it, love? You and your boss. Another
top-level conference. Feel my arm. All his travel arrangements
at your fingertips. Every hitch anticipated by his unobtrusive
Girl Friday. I love this girl. I live for this girl. Feel my arm.

LINDA: (*Still looking at the letter*) Preserve what?

MAM: A close-knit community. The society of the streets. They
want to know why we're so happy.

DAD: Feel my arm. It's irrelevant to you, Linda. You triumphed
over all that. You transcended it.

LINDA: Where's my suitcase? I'm leaving.

DAD: You don't need a suitcase, Linda. An overnight bag's all
you want. A change of clothes and a few simple accessories.
Europe these days, it's only like the next street.

LINDA: I'm leaving. How many more times?

MAM: Leaving? Why?

LINDA: I'm going to Saudi Arabia. (LINDA *goes upstairs.*)

DAD: Saudi Arabia! That's the way with Linda. One minute she's
here, next minute she's flying over the Red Sea.

LINDA: (*Off*) Where's my suitcase?

MAM: Look on top of our wardrobe. She sounds to be leaving
for good.

DAD: Business trip. Moment's notice. Rooms booked at the local
Intercontinental Hotel. Prawn cocktail and steak diane in her
room, followed by early bed so as to be fresh and alert at her
boss's elbow for the first round of negotiations in the

morning. It won't take her two minutes to pack. Always travels light does Linda. Got it down to a fine art. Toothbrush and briefcase, that's all she needs.

(*At this point* LINDA *comes in with a large suitcase and an equally large pink teddy bear or dog.*)

Planning to be away long, love? When is the duration of the conference?

LINDA: What conference? I'm going to Saudi Arabia. To live.

MAM: You live here, Linda. This is your home.

LINDA: This? It's a pigsty.

MAM: We're your parents.

LINDA: Yes. Fat Pig One and Fat Pig Two.

MAM: Ignore that, love. She's probably menstruating.

DAD: It's not very commodious here, I agree, but it'll be different once we're into the maisonette.

MAM: The bus service is tip top and you'll have your own room with washbasin *en suite*.

LINDA: I'm going to Saudi Arabia.

DAD: You can't. It's sons that migrate; daughters, they're supposed to live round the corner. You can confirm that. You're the sociologist.

(MS CRAIG *is blank.*)

Nod, you blank bugger.

LINDA: Who says I am your daughter anyway?

DAD: Linda!

MAM: Course you're our daughter: I bought you those slippers.

LINDA: They've brought me up, I grant you, but it would take more than that to convince me this is my mother and father. As such.

DAD: Linda. You've never voiced these doubts before.

LINDA: I've never had an independent witness before.

MAM: But we have pictures of you as a baby. On a rug. I should have kept the rug. That would have proved it.

DAD: You've staggered me a bit, Linda. I've to some extent idolized you. I must be your father. I've given you that much affection.

LINDA: I contemplated having a blood test, but I was told it wouldn't be conclusive, and even if it was it wouldn't convince me. Though I could modify my position to this extent: one of you may be my parent but definitely not both.

DAD: You're my daughter right enough. I recognize my dogged determination. My optimism and will to win.

MAM: She's got my hair. Her hair's the split image of mine. Her eyes are the same colour.

DAD: (*Contemptuously*) Blue.

MAM: She's got my skin.

LINDA: Your skin, lady? Is that your skin? I should know.

DAD: No, she's my girl, this one. Set her sights on something she wants and she goes all out to get it. I was like that once. My girl.

MAM: And mine.

(*Silence*)

And mine, Dad.

(DAD *doesn't answer.* MAM *weeps.*)

LINDA: Do you remember having me?

MAM: I remember having somebody. I had a lot of pain. I remember the pain.

LINDA: What intrigues me is who the other person was. I imagine it must have been somebody prominent in the world of sport or entertainment. A tycoon possibly. Someone with bags of personality at any rate. Quite frankly it wouldn't surprise me if it was somebody extra-terrestrial.

DAD: Don't be so daft, Linda. What would I be doing with somebody extra-terrestrial?

MAM: You must be our daughter: we love you.

LINDA: Love. You're always on about love. I don't want love. I want consumer goods.

(LINDA *goes upstairs for a moment.* DAD *sits in flabbergasted silence while* MS CRAIG *writes slowly.*

The ensuing conversation is partly shouted up the stairs.)

DAD: Why Saudi Arabia?

LINDA: (*Off*) It could be Kuwait. Plans aren't finalized yet.

MAM: You'd be a fool to leave Leeds. (*To* MS CRAIG.) It's a tip-top shopping centre now they've secluded the traffic. A pedestrians' paradise. There's some grand shops, people come from all over. (*Pause. To* LINDA.) I saw a very reasonable little costume in Lewis's. (*Pause*) The new precinct's gorgeous. It's all climate controlled. It's a godsend in inclement weather. Tell her, Dad. It has the biggest Boots outside Manchester.

DAD: There won't be a Boots in Kuwait.

LINDA: There will. There'll be everything there soon. Boots, Littlewoods. C. & A. They're queuing up.

MAM: Not climate controlled.

LINDA: No need to control it. It's hot.

DAD: Turning your back on all this love.

MAM: They have some right bonny little handbags in Schofields.

LINDA: I'm going to bury the past. And everyone that goes with it.

DAD: We're getting on, Linda.

MAM: Our idea was that you'd look after us in our old age. We thought you'd be bobbing in and out like daughters do. You can't do that from . . . where is it you're going? Sweden?

LINDA: I have my own young life to lead.

DAD: What will happen to us?

LINDA: You're going into the horrible new flats.

MAM: What if we can't manage?

LINDA: Contact your social worker.

MAM: We don't have a social worker. Do we?

(LINDA *should play whenever possible to* MS CRAIG.)

LINDA: Then do what everybody else does: go into a home.

MAM: We don't want to go into a home.

LINDA: Why? There's some nice homes now. Big places on the outskirts, standing in their own grounds. Drives, shrubbery, everything. One even has a lake. Feed the ducks.

DAD: Who'll come and see us.

LINDA: All sorts come. These voluntary groups. The Variety Club comes. Lions come. Unemployed school leavers come. Old folks in homes these days, they're inundated with visitors. You won't have a moment to yourselves. I can send you a postcard now and again to pin up on the door of your locker. (*To* MS CRAIG.) They provide them with lockers now. They've got much more enlightened in that respect.

MAM: I'll make a cup of tea. Oh Dad, Dad! (*She goes into the scullery.*)

DAD: Linda.

LINDA: What?

DAD: With all due respect to your mother, Linda, she is the imposter.

(LINDA *is in and out packing so* DAD *is talking to her and to* MS CRAIG.)

She doesn't take after her Mam for a start. Linda's not swilling and scrubbing and keeping the place straight. She's like me, devil may care. I'm the genuine parent. No question. But when it comes to who her mother was I'm a bit stumped. I think Linda's right, it's got to be someone who mirrors her qualities, someone with poise and bags of get up and go, somebody famous. And I have to admit my contacts with the famous have been few and far between. We had the Princess Royal down to the works once to open a new canteen. She half-paused at an adjoining table and expressed interest to some fellow workmates in the colour of the formica top, but that's as far as it went. Then I had some contact with Mrs Somebody-Something, a famous Dutch sprinter.

LINDA: A Dutch spinster?

DAD: No, love. Sprinter. She won the Olympics once before you were born. Not a particularly good-looking woman but the personality very well defined. She ran past the end of the street once in pursuit of some charity thing and I remember thinking 'Well, there's an opportunity here if I want to take it.' But to my mind the most likely candidate was one of the Rank starlets. You won't remember them. They were starlets for Rank, generally girls with large busts who'd been in films then went round the provinces officiating at functions. This one was Dawn something or something Dawn. She epitomized glamour.

LINDA: Glamour?

DAD: I met her when she was presiding over the gala opening of a discount warehouse in converted premises formerly a church. We went along for sentimental reasons . . . we'd got married there . . . and also because we were crying out for a bit of underfelt for the stairs. I know I engaged this Rank lady in conversation. I have her autograph on the back of a

B   33

bill for felt underlay. It's upstairs somewhere if your so-called mother hasn't thrown it away. Whether anything actually transpired I can't say with any certainty. I have a very clear picture in my mind of something happening between us. The point is, Linda, I think you're right. That isn't your mother. That woman. You've no ties in that direction. Me, it's different. We're one and the same, you and me.

And the way I've been thinking is that with my experience in the Western Desert I'm actually cut out for Kuwait. I revel in the heat whereas your mother (her in there), she hates it. I've been begging her for years to go to Torquay only she says she was smothered at Scarborough. So where are you? Kuwait would suit my arm. The feeling would be back in no time. What do you say, Linda?

LINDA: I wasn't listening.

DAD: There's that many things I could do for you. Little jobs. I could keep your cosmetics ship-shape for instance. Not allow those nasty deposits to form round the top of your nail-varnish bottle . . . keep your mascara brushes soft and yielding . . . always have a point ready on your eyebrow pencils. Let me come, Linda.

MAM: (*Returning*) How will you make a living? You'll have to go out to work.

LINDA: Work? I shall never have to work again. I'm getting married.

MAM: Married! Oh, Linda. Why didn't you say? I'm so happy. She's getting married, Dad. Our Linda's getting married. I thought she was just going out there on spec but it's wedding bells!

DAD: I don't want her to get married. She's not ready for marriage. I've yet to meet the man that's good enough for our Linda.

MAM: Who will it be?

DAD: Kuwait? It will be one of these international oil men.

MAM: An oil man? You need a degree for that. Some form of higher education anyway. Our Linda's marrying somebody with qualifications.

(LINDA *returns*.)

When's the wedding?

LINDA: This afternoon. At least the civil ceremony. When we get to Saudi Arabia they have the religious ceremony where they slit the throat of a goat.

MAM: A goat. Oh. We've always been Church of England. Still it's nice when they believe anything at all these days. And I suppose the animals are more used to it out there. He's not an oil man then?

LINDA: Oil man? He's a prince.

MAM: A *prince*. Linda!

DAD: He's not coloured?

LINDA: Probably. I haven't seen him yet.

MAM: You haven't seen him? It's not love then?

LINDA: It might be. He's seen pictures of me.

MAM: Oh, well. It may ripen into love. These arranged things often do. Royalty it often ripens into love. You read about it. King Hussein married like that and his ripened into love. Even some of ours marry like that and it always ripens into love.

DAD: Where did he see these pictures of you?

LINDA: They were shown him by a business associate. He's sending a car.

MAM: A car, Dad! A prince is sending a car for our Linda!

LINDA: Only the bugger's late.

DAD: There won't be a car. They don't send cars for lasses who answer adverts.

LINDA: Who said I answered an advert? They're sending a car. They're sending a sodding car.

DAD: None of your secretary talk here. Who is he, then, this so-called prince? Why does he want to marry you?

LINDA: Why does anybody want to marry anybody? Why did you want to marry her?

DAD: I can't remember.

MAM: Love, wasn't it?

DAD: Candid photographs, were they? Full length?

LINDA: I was holding a bicycle and looking apprehensive. They were very tasteful.

MAM: Not taken at your desk, then? Sitting at your typewriter?

LINDA: No. I have been photographed at a desk. Sitting on a typewriter.

MAM: On it? How unusual.

DAD: Can I see them?

   (LINDA *ignores this*.)

   Getting all this down, are you?

MAM: I'd forgotten you. I was being utterly natural. Though this isn't normal. It's not every day Linda gets married and goes off to . . . where is it you're going, love?

LINDA: Saudi Arabia.

DAD: She's not going to Saudi Arabia.

LINDA: I bloody am.

DAD: Over my dead body.

MAM: You see. As soon as I draw their attention to you they start showing off.

DAD: You've been had. It's another con. You're always being conned. There won't be a car. Resign yourself. This is where you belong. At home with us. Feel my arm.

LINDA: No car? What's this then?

   (LINDA *looks through one window,* MRS CRAVEN *with her*.)

MAM: (*Awestruck*) Is that it?

LINDA: That's just the bonnet.

MAM: Come look, Dad. It's that long, I can't even see the front of it.

   (DAD *looks out of a different window*.)

DAD: I can't see the back.

LINDA: So now do you believe me?

MAM: I never doubted it. It's your Dad. He's been a sceptic ever since we were first married. What is he like, your fiancé? Quiet? Some of them can be very nicely spoken.

LINDA: I haven't *met* him.

MAM: He must have a good job, car like that.

DAD: Nobody has jobs in Saudi Arabia. They just sit over a hole in the ground and put it in cans. That's not a job.

MAM: What?

DAD: Oil, you flaming naff head.

MAM: I'm more easy in my mind, now that I know that he's a prince and seen the car. You've done very well, Linda. The girl King Hussein married was only a shop assistant, though very vivacious apparently. Makes me wish we had a car.

36

LINDA: You wouldn't want a car like that. It's armour plated.

MAM: Vandals?

LINDA: Assassination.

DAD: I couldn't drive a car. Not with my arm. It'd have to be specially adapted.

LINDA: It is specially adapted: it's got a flame thrower.

MAM: Oh, that's unusual.

LINDA: One touch on the button and you're both dead. Burnt to a cinder.

MAM: Well there's all sorts of gadgets now, but if it gets you from point A to point B that's all you want.

LINDA: He's probably got it trained on you at this very moment.

MAM: Really? What will they think of next? (MAM *waves*.) That's not your fiancé driving it?

LINDA: That's the chauffeur.

MAM: He's English anyway.

LINDA: English? He's got a degree in mechanical engineering.

MAM: If he's got a degree why don't you fetch him in. He could perhaps do with a cup of tea.

LINDA: If I even looked at him they would have to chop his hands off at the elbow. Honour.

MAM: Your Uncle Graham was a bit like that. Someone looked at Thelma once and he threw them through a plate-glass window. But that wasn't religion. It was drink.

LINDA: I'll just go and have a word with him. (LINDA *goes out*.)

MAM: She'll probably have a swimming-pool.

DAD: In the car, possibly.

MAM: A cocktail bar.

DAD: Sauna.

MAM: I'd like a car with toilet facilities. W.C. Wash-hand basin. With facilities like that there'd be no need to get out of the car at all. The chauffeur looks nice. I've a sneaking wish our Linda was marrying him. Come and look at the car, love. (MS CRAIG *doesn't move*.)
It's all part of the picture. Happiness!
(MS CRAIG *gets up slowly and goes to one window and looks. Goes to the other. Sits down. Makes a slight note*.)

DAD: You don't ride in cars like that, madam.

MAM: I knew a cinema-manager a bit like him. Refined-looking. I can always pick out people who know what the word suffering means. He's coming in.

(LINDA *comes in with the handsome brute of a chauffeur,* HERITAGE.)

LINDA: Heritage wondered if you would like to look round the car and have a cocktail from the cabinet.

MAM: A cocktail. Why, what time is it? Thanks very much.

DAD: I'm stopping here with Linda. She'll be leaving us soon. Every minute is precious. (*He doesn't move.*)

MAM: You stunt me, Dad. Here's an unlooked-for opportunity for cocktails in the back of a Rolls Royce and you turn your nose up.

DAD: Linda.

LINDA: Go and have a flaming cocktail.

MAM: Are you coming, love, or are you staying to observe Linda? (MS CRAIG *doesn't move.*)

This isn't normal, of course. It's only once in a blue moon we have cocktails in the back of a Rolls Royce.

(MAM *and* DAD *go out, with* HERITAGE, MAM *singing 'Waltz of My Heart' (Novello,* The Dancing Years).)

LINDA: I shall be glad to see the back of this place. I can't wait to open the curtains in a morning and see minarets. (*She stands in front of* MS CRAIG.) Hello. Don't you have a little word for me then?

(*She laughs and is stroking* MS CRAIG'*s face when* HERITAGE *returns. She leaves her hand on* MS CRAIG'*s face for a moment before turning to him.*

She and HERITAGE *embrace passionately.*

This continues for a few moments. MS CRAIG *watches impassively.*)

LINDA: She's watching you, Brian. She's watching you kissing me. I can see her watching us. Can you?

HERITAGE No. I want to see her. I want to see her watching me.

LINDA: Get round in front of the mirror then. Get me in front of the mirror. Can you see her?

HERITAGE: Edge round.

LINDA: Oh, Brian. Can you see her?

HERITAGE: I can see her. The dirty bitch. She's just watching.
　　The dirty cow.
LINDA: Brian.
HERITAGE: What?
LINDA: I . . . I can't see her now.
HERITAGE: I want you to see her.
LINDA: I can't.
HERITAGE: I want to see you, seeing her, seeing me.
LINDA: We need another mirror. (*She looks round for one.*) That's
　　typical of this place: no amenities.
HERITAGE: I like her legs. Though she hasn't got much in the
　　way of tits.
LINDA: Course not. If you've got tits you don't work for the
　　Council; you get yourself into the private sector. Like me.
　　Brian.
HERITAGE: Linda.
　　(*They fall on the floor in front of* MS CRAIG *who moves very
　　slightly to accommodate them.*)
　　I can see right up her legs.
LINDA: You can see right up mine, if you want.
HERITAGE: Yes, only she doesn't want me to see up hers. Taking
　　it all in, aren't you? Watching my every move. Watching my
　　hands. Oh, yes.
　　(HERITAGE *starts to get* LINDA's *knickers down.*)
　　What's matter?
LINDA: I've gone off it.
HERITAGE: Well I bloody haven't.
LINDA: Well I bloody have. On the living-room floor? We're not
　　animals. Don't imagine this is the norm, coitus on the
　　carpet. I'm more on the shy side. You can't get me out of
　　my shell normally but it's with being on the eve of marriage:
　　there's a lot of unreleased tension. Mind you I knew he was
　　only after one thing when I saw him eyeing me in the
　　rear-view mirror. Kindly rejoin your vehicle.
HERITAGE: Sod you, madam.
LINDA: Don't you madam me. You're an employee.
HERITAGE: So are you.
LINDA: I am a personal secretary. I shall see my husband to be is

39

informed of your conduct. It falls far short of the professional standards he is entitled to expect as a visitor to these shores and I hope he saws your scrotum off. He can, you know, in Saudi Arabia. They're a law unto themselves. And send them two inside, else there won't be a maraschino cherry left. And Heritage . . .

HERITAGE: Yes, madam.

LINDA: The luggage.

HERITAGE: Cow.

LINDA: Whatever happened to our tradition of service?

(HERITAGE *goes*.)

Nice of you to take an interest in the parents, so-called. I'm under intolerable pressure sometimes. I can't see what they have to live for, quite frankly. People do cling on, don't they? My problem is: I hate my loved ones. Folks do these days, I read it in *Readers' Digest*. They either love them, which means they hate them. Else they hate them, which means they love them. Of course most people keep up a façade. Only I can't, I'm just too honest. Smoke? Very wise. I'm going to give up when I get to Saudi Arabia. Do you believe in reincarnation? I do. I think that's why I can't get on with those two, they're so many turns behind me. They were probably insects last time round, whereas me, I get the feeling I'm quite advanced. I've been something Egyptian, I know that for a fact, some quite high-up handmaiden . . . I'm going back a few thousand years now. I know I was once waiting on in the temple in a ritual that culminated in human sacrifice. Another time I came over with the Vikings. As a man, of course. Sex is irrelevant in the great chain of being. Last time I think I was twins and died on the guillotine. It's fascinating when you go into it. I've read a great deal about it in paperback.

(MAM *and* DAD *are returning*.)

MAM: Nice car, Linda. The only comparable vehicle I've been in was at your Grandma's funeral. Only that didn't have a cocktail cabinet. I liked the absence of piped music. That was very tasteful. I shall save my cocktail stick as a memento.

LINDA: Right, I'm off.

MAM: Where are you going?

DAD: Linda. Aren't you going to kiss your father?

MAM: Aren't you going to kiss your mother? (Where is it she's going?)

LINDA: Saudi bloody Arabia.

MAM: Saudi Arabia. (*Weeping*) I never thought I'd have to kiss somebody goodbye who was going to Saudi Arabia.

DAD: You love us, don't you, Linda?

MAM: Course she loves us. Will it be Concorde?

LINDA: I expect so.

MAM: Fancy, Dad, our only daughter flying at twice the speed of sound plus as much champagne as she can drink.

DAD: You'll not like it. Women out there, they're rubbish.

MAM: That's their own women. They'll treat you like a goddess and if they don't you want to come straight back. With the customs being different I don't suppose they'll send out bits of wedding cake.

LINDA: No, but I'll send you some of the goat. (*She laughs.*)

MAM: Bless her. She's just trying to put a face on it, she'll be in floods of tears once she's round the corner. Maybe when you've settled in we could come out by the overland route and have a fortnight together somewhere at the seaside. Say goodbye to the young lady. Come on, Dad. Let's wave her off. (MAM *and* DAD *get up and go outside.*

MS CRAIG *remains sitting for a moment, then gets up and walks slowly round the room. She stops in front of the fireplace and looks at the mantelpiece.*)

MS CRAIG: One clock in light oak, presented to Mam's father after forty years with Greenwood and Batley. Stopped; the key lost.

A wooden candlestick that's never seen a candle. A tube of ointment for a skin complaint that cleared up after one application. An airmail letter, two years old, announcing the death of a cousin in Perth, Western Australia, the stamp torn off. Two half-crowns not cashed at decimalization because Mam read in the *Evening Post* that one day they would be priceless. Four old halfpennies kept on the same principle. A dry Biro.

Various reminders on the backs of envelopes. 'Pension, Thursday', 'Dad's pills', 'Gone down the road. Dinner on'. And, starkly, 'Gas'. A rubber band. Three plastic clips from the package of a new shirt, kept by Dad with the idea it will save wasting money on paper clips. Not that he ever does waste money on paper clips.

Three tuppeny-halfpenny stamps.

A packet of nasturtium seeds on offer with some custard powder. A newspaper-cutting recording the conviction for shoplifting of the wife of the local vicar, saved to send to relatives in Canada. Dad's last appointment card at the Infirmary and two grey aspirins.

Altar, noticeboard, medicine chest, cemetery. A shrine laden with the relics of the recent past and a testimonial to the faith that one day the world will turn and the past come back into its own and there will be a restoration. The coinage will make sense once more, letters again cost twopence halfpenny and life return to its old ways. On that day the nasturtiums will be planted, the half-crowns spent, the skin complaint will recur and the ointment be applied once more to the affected part. The Biro will flow again, the second cousin in Toronto will be informed at last of the conviction of the vicar's wife and on that day the key will be found and the clock strike.

(MS CRAIG *hears* MAM *and* DAD *returning and sits down*.)

MAM: She's gone. (*Pause*) Only us now.

DAD: Be off, you. We don't want you here now Linda's gone.

MAM: No, Dad. She's not to go. She's all right where she is. We shall be wanting a bit of company.

(*To the strains of 'Fly Home Little Heart'* (*Novello*, King's Rhapsody) MS CRAIG *slowly takes out a cigarette and lights it.* MAM *puts an ash-tray within range of her chair. Pause*.)

MAM: Where is it our Linda's gone? (*Pause*) Dad!

DAD: Feel my arm.

(MAM's *recorded voice is heard singing 'Fly Home Little Heart' as the curtain falls.*)

ACT TWO

MAM's *voice is heard singing 'Love is My Reason for Living'*
(*Novello*, Perchance to Dream) *as the curtain rises on* DAD *and*
MS CRAIG *alone.*
Long pause.

DAD: The phrase 'no love lost' has always puzzled me. As in the
sentence 'There was no love lost between me and her.' What
does that mean? Does it mean that the love between the
persons concerned was so precious they could not bear to
spill a single drop? And thus no love went to waste. Taking
love as some kind of liquid. I'm thinking of me and Linda.
Or does 'no love lost' mean there was no love? None
whatsoever. He didn't waste any love on her or she on him,
so none was lost and they both hung onto their quota.
(*Pause*)
And 'Butter wouldn't melt in her mouth.' What the fuck
does that mean? Somebody could be sat there looking as if
butter wouldn't melt in her mouth and I wouldn't recognize
it. I should miss it.
(*Pause*)
A woman came round with leaflets once. Special offer. Dry
cleaning. Eiderdowns re-covered. Very reasonable. I had her
on that table. Youngish woman. White boots. Butter melted
in her mouth, one way and another.
(*Pause*)
She'll forget what she's gone for. She writes it down but she
forgets she's written it down. She goes out for a bit of
something tasty for the tea and comes back with toilet-rolls.
We'll be found starved to death and the house stuffed with
toilet-rolls.

43

(*Pause*)

I'm conversing but don't be misled. I'm still inconsolable over Linda. The bitch. My own daughter. I've invested so much love in that girl over the years. Saudi Arabia. Well, I'm writing it off. As from today. It was a bad investment and I'm disappointed. But I'm not going to let it get in the way of my new life. I'm going to start mixing again. I haven't mixed properly since my accident. Now there's going to be an alteration. Once we get into the flats I shall make a point of getting to know the other occupants. Get on dropping-in terms. Drop in on them, have them drop in on me. For coffee, for instance. I shall have a real shot at being the life and soul of the party and live more like you see in the adverts. I've never been a good mixer but I've discovered the secret now. It's to take an interest in other people. That's what makes people like you. If you take an interest in them. I've read several articles in different magazines and they all say the same: 'Take an interest in other people.' I tell you I'm going to be a changed man.

(*Pause*)

Have you any hobbies?

Do you do anything in your spare time?

You're probably a person of wide interests.

Those are questions normally guaranteed to break the ice.

(*The ice remains unbroken.*)

Remember I asked anyway. Make a note. (*She doesn't.*) I can't tell you how much I welcome this opportunity of talking to you alone. She confuses matters. I hope you noticed that as soon as she went we really started to hit it off. It was like that with the boy. My son so-called. He was in perpetual partnership with his mam. I never got near. I would have liked to have put my stamp on him but I never even got to take him to a football match. We would very likely have got on like a house on fire on our own only she was always putting her spoke in, making out she and him were the big duo. He'd have loved me, given the chance, I know. I don't see how he could have stopped himself.

(*Pause*)

44

Are you tall?
(*A moment, then* MS CRAIG *stands up.*)
I can't see.
(*She approaches.*)
You are tall.
(*She stands in front of him.*)
Show me your hand.
(*She slowly holds out her hand.*)
It's a smooth hand. It's a big hand. It's smooth only it's big.
He'd never hold my hand when he was little. Always her
hand. I had to force him. What would you say if I asked to
hold your hand? (*He takes her hand.*) It's a father's right.
It's normal.
(MS CRAIG *looks down at him and he up at her at which point*
there is a loud bang on the door.
She unhurriedly sits down again.
A voice comes through the letter-box. It is young, wheedling
and intimidating.)

ANTHONY: Hello, Grandad. It's me, Grandad.

DAD: I'm not your Grandad. Go away.

ANTHONY: I want to come in, Grandad.

DAD: You can't come in. I've got somebody with me.

ANTHONY: Grandad's lying. She's gone shopping. Grandad.
Grandad.

DAD: I'm not his Grandad. How could I be his Grandad? What?

ANTHONY: I've a new book to show you.

DAD: I'm not in the mood.

ANTHONY: It's a good one.

DAD: He gets these books out. War books mainly. Rommel,
Monty. The war in the desert seen in terms of overall
strategy.

ANTHONY: Pictures of twat. Grandad.

DAD: I'm not his Grandad.

ANTHONY: You'll like this one. (*He kicks the door.*)

DAD: He'll get bored in a bit. They do get bored his generation.
We never got bored.
(MR CRAVEN *takes a zinc bath from behind the door and puts it*
across the threshold.)

He's a hooligan. He's been sent away once or twice but he persistently absconds. He's out of control. He sometimes has green hair.

(*The letter-box opens and* ANTHONY *proceeds to piss through it into the zinc bath.*)

That's one of his favourite tricks, pissing through the letter-box. It's another thing that makes me look forward to the new flats. They're a different class of people there. And the letter-boxes are much higher up.

(*Another bang.*)

ANTHONY: A book, Grandad.

DAD: At school they're not interested in books. The teachers can't get them to look at books. I can't let him in on your account. He has these boots somebody bought him. Steel-tipped. They don't function as boots. They don't buy them for boots, because they're hard-wearing, they buy them to kick people to death with. The manufacturers want reporting.

ANTHONY: Books.

(MS CRAIG *gets up.*)

DAD: Where are you going? Sit down. Where've you got to? Come away from that door. You'll have him inside. Leave that.

(MS CRAIG *unlatches the door and sits down again, unhurriedly. The door opens and* ANTHONY *comes in slowly, calm and smiling.*)

ANTHONY: Hello, Grandad.

(*He is about sixteen.*)

DAD: His hair's generally dyed.

(ANTHONY *has left the door open and a youngish man* (GREGORY) *comes in, notebook in hand, and leans against the wall watching.*)

Who's this? Who're you?

ANTHONY: It's Gregory, Grandad. It's my friend Gregory. He's attached to me. I'm being studied.

DAD: Studied? You've just pissed through our letter-box!

ANTHONY: I had to do that. I have to act normally. I'm not supposed to behave. It's not like probation. I do what I want. Unless I do just what I want, it's useless. Isn't it, Gregory?

46

(GREGORY *is impassive as is* MS CRAIG.)

DAD: Does yours talk?

ANTHONY: He says 'fuck' now and again, but in a very natural way.

DAD: That's an earring he's got. In my day it was tattooes. Now it's earrings and coloured hair. Some of them dress up in smart little suits: they're the worst of all.

ANTHONY: I want to show you a book.

DAD: I don't want to see no book. A lad of your age. You ought to be outside playing football instead of stuck inside reading books. He's not a bad boy. He's run me no end of errands in the past. When they've done dyeing their hair and putting earrings in they're just lads same as we were. See, get yourself one or two crisps. (*He tries to snatch the book.*)

ANTHONY: I hope you're taking note of this carry-on. Under ordinary circumstances he would have no hesitation. This isn't the real him. You're making him shy.

DAD: You bugger.

ANTHONY: Dad and I share a common interest in the female figure, nude for preference.

DAD: It's a lie.

(ANTHONY *puts* DAD'*s stick out of reach.*)

ANTHONY: There's genuine affection here though that may be hard to credit. It is not a lie.

DAD: Young man, help me.

ANTHONY: Gregory can't help you. It's not a part of his brief. Gregory's brief is to watch me. Stay with it, Greg. What say we adhere to our usual practice, Dad. I browse through until we hit upon something of mutual interest, fair enough? She's boring for a start. You're not looking, Grandad. You've got to look.

DAD: Go away. Showing me up.

ANTHONY: You should see us, Greg. These publications are our constant study. Not looking, Grandad.

DAD: It's true I do see them now and again. But they come from a very respectable newsagent's. There are sometimes articles about people's philosophies. How they got started in life. That's what interests the discerning reader.

ANTHONY: I don't think we like her, do we? Nor the usual

47

Portuguese waiter with his obligatory slack dick. No thanks.

DAD: Footballers give their thoughts. Prominent businessmen discuss free enterprise. Famous novelists tell you about drinks. There's a whole world here if you know how to acquire it.

ANTHONY: Nothing so far, but I am about to turn the vital page. *Watch*, you old sod. Look. (*He covers the face of the model.*) Now. Those tits ring a bell? You're not looking. Look. *Watch*.

DAD: No. No.

ANTHONY: (*Reading*) 'When it comes to changing a wheel our Norma can beat a man hands down.'

'Norma, who hails from Southport has no trouble putting her hand on the jack but is a bit puzzled what to do with it.'

'Ah, well, next time we have a blow-out we hope Norma's in the vicinity.'

Who's that, then, Grandad?

DAD: I don't know.

ANTHONY: They've got her name wrong. Her name's not Norma. Her name's Linda.

DAD: It never is. Our Linda's got brown hair. That one's a blonde. And Linda doesn't come from Southport.

ANTHONY: A wig, Dad. She's wearing a wig.

DAD: Our Linda knows nothing about cars.

ANTHONY: It's Linda.

DAD: Linda's a personal secretary.

ANTHONY: You old tosser. Your own daughter and you don't recognize her.

DAD: It's not her. I'd know if it was her.

ANTHONY: There's something wrong with your brain, Dad, if you don't recognize your own daughter. I'm going to have to lift up your steel plate and find out.

DAD: No. Leave my head alone. Stop him. Help me.

(GREGORY *and* MS CRAIG *rise*.)

ANTHONY: Now, Greg. Remember your brief. Knock, knock. Anybody there.

(*He bangs on* DAD's *head*. DAD *slumps in the chair*.)

Shit. He's passed out. Dad? Come on, Dad. Come on. Joke over.

Well whose fault was that? You saw what happened. I was

making this big effort to behave normally and he wasn't
even trying. He was allowing his conduct to be influenced by
the presence of onlookers. He gets bashful, resists and
naturally he gets hurt. I'm really depressed now. I like him.
Up to a point we're intimate friends, only when somebody's
watching the barriers go up. Though why I can't imagine.
What is there to be ashamed of? We're all human basically.
(ANTHONY *shows* GREGORY *the magazine then goes back.*)
He's not coming round. Wake up, Wilfred! He doesn't look
well. What about it, Greg?
(GREGORY *comes over slowly, looks at* MR CRAVEN *and says
nothing. He is back in his position when* MAM *comes in with
her shopping.*)

MAM: I'd forgotten we'd got company. I couldn't remember what
it was I went for but I got one or two things that'll come in.
Our usual greengrocer's been knocked down. It was a
pleasant little parade: butchers, confectioners, ladies'
knitwear shop. Catered for just about everything and made a
nice little outing. Now there's one shop selling used office
furniture and the rest is a garden centre. They want their
heads examining. Has Anthony been behaving himself?
Hello, Anthony. (What's happened to your green hair?)
Hello? (*To* GREGORY.) The bulldozers are knocking on. No
trace of the Grasmeres. Dad asleep? You asleep, Dad?
(MAM *takes the shopping, toilet-rolls, into the scullery.*
ANTHONY *jerks his head to* GREGORY *and goes.* GREGORY *pauses.*)

GREGORY: (*To* MS CRAIG) That bugger looks dead to me.
Something anyway.
(GREGORY *shakes his head and maybe ruffles* ANTHONY'*s hair as
they go.*)

MAM: (*From the scullery*) I've just remembered I went for a tin of
salmon. My mother went like this, you know. She lost her
memory. I didn't see anybody I knew. I got a bit of a smile
from one woman but that's all; there weren't many people
about. They're curtailing the buses now. Scarcely a building
as far as the eye can see and then they say we're short of
open spaces. (*Coming in.*) Are you all right, Dad? You
haven't been having an argument? He's not sulking again?

Sat there with your mouth open. Dad. *Dad.* DAD. I think he's had a funny do. Dad. Wake up. He's had a turn. Have you noticed anything?

(MS CRAIG *is impassive.*)

Say something. There must be a case for waiving the rules now and again. Dad. Dad. It's Mam. Wilf! Wilf!

(*Pause.* MAM *goes out hurriedly.*

MS CRAIG *gets up slowly and goes over to* MR CRAVEN. *She looks at him without touching him, then picks up* ANTHONY'S *magazine and glances at it. She hears* MAM *returning and goes back unhurriedly to her chair.*

MRS CRAVEN *returns with* MRS CLEGG, *her next-door neighbour, a woman of the same age and some pretensions to refinement.* MRS CLEGG *takes in* MS CRAIG *and listens to* MR CRAVEN'S *chest. As she is doing so another observer* (ADRIAN) *comes in, pad and pencil in hand and hovers about watching her.*)

MAM: Has he gone?

(MRS CLEGG *listens to* MR CRAVEN'S *chest, while watching* MS CRAIG *to whom she addresses sotto voce remarks.*)

MRS CLEGG (*Mouthing*) How do you do?

MAM: He's not gone, Nora?

MRS CLEGG: Mrs Clegg. From next door.

MAM: He was right as rain when I went out. Has he gone?

MRS CLEGG: (*Still addressing* MS CRAIG) They always turn to me. First sign of a crisis, it's 'fetch Nora'.

MAM: I'd call Dr Sillitoe but I'd want to change him first. And this place is upside down.

MRS CLEGG: You don't want him trailing all the way over here on a wild-goose chase. And you can't ring up. The kiosk's been vandalized. The insides have been ripped out again. I'd rip their insides out. He's got a good colour and he's not cold. If he has gone we've only just missed him. Was he constipated at all?

MAM: I'm not sure. It's not something he'd ever discuss.

MRS CLEGG: Is he dead, that's the question? We could burn some feathers under his nose, that's a traditional method. Have you got a pillow?

MAM: Yes, but they're all foam filled.

MRS CLEGG: With polystyrene? Burn that and it gives off a deadly poison.

MAM: Nora, what's happening to the world?

MRS CLEGG: I don't know. I'd castrate them.

MAM: Would he help? (*Indicating the new observer.*)

MRS CLEGG: Out of the question.

MAM: Mine won't even converse.

MRS CLEGG: Nor mine. But if he did I've a feeling he'd be very nicely spoken.

MAM: But Nora is he dead? Till I know I'm not sure what to do. Should I be showing grief? Do I mourn or what? I don't want to jump the gun. Isn't there somebody at the Council we could ring?

MRS CLEGG: No. (*Sotto voce.*) Not with them watching us. We've got to manage. Not fall back on outside agencies.

MAM: Is this death? I'd like an official view.

MRS CLEGG: Be brave, Connie. I think you must resign yourself to the fact that your beloved hubby has passed on.

MAM: Oh, Wilf. Are you sure?

MRS CLEGG: Ninety-nine per cent.

MAM: Wilf! Wilf! He never used to call me by name. Never Connie. Always Mam. Never my name except one stage when he used to call it out when ejaculating. I think I was meant to be touched. When he saw it cut no ice he desisted. I don't think he's said my name since.

MRS CLEGG: Now. The first thing to do is to lay him out in the customary manner, wash the body and dress it in the clean clothes traditionally set aside for this purpose. (*All this is directed towards the observers.*)

MAM: Can't Chippendales do that? The undertakers.

MRS CLEGG: Chippendales has changed hands. It's now a patio-paving centre. There is no Chippendales.

MAM: No Chippendales? Oh, Nora.

MRS CLEGG: I know. I'd bastinado them.

MAM: I'm not sure he's got a clean vest. I was going to wash it. That was one of the jobs I'd got lined up for today. What must they think? My mother could have done all this by instinct.

MRS CLEGG: You'll have the coffin here, of course. Not at the Chapel of Rest. So impersonal. You want to be grateful it happened at home. I had Clifford at home.

MAM: It's a good job we haven't got into the horrible new flats. They wouldn't get coffins into the lift.

MRS CLEGG: Another example of shortsighted planning. I'd strangle them at birth.

MAM: I keep forgetting what it is they're looking for.

MRS CLEGG: Survivors, that's what they're looking for. People who haven't gone under. I don't think I disappointed them. It's a nice change for me. I haven't had somebody dogging my every footstep since Clifford died.

MAM: Will it get written up?

MRS CLEGG: I imagine in the form of a report.

(MAM *goes into the scullery for some water.*)

I know I shall figure, albeit anonymously. We're a dying breed, women like me. I could probably deliver a baby if I was ever called upon and I can administer an enema at a moment's notice. Birth or death I'm an asset at any bedside. I don't dislike this carpet.

MAM: (*Returning*) I forget, you see, that's my trouble. I think I'd have more of the qualities they're looking for if only I could remember. My mother was like that.

They're writing all this down and none of it's normal.

Cocktails in a Rolls Royce. Linda flying off in Concorde and now Dad dead. None of it run of the mill.

MRS CLEGG: You're lucky to have had such an action-packed day. I had some baking to do and one or two things to rinse through but nothing dramatic. Nothing to stretch me, nothing that demanded the whole of my personality.

MAM: You're getting some spin-off from this though.

MRS CLEGG: And that is what they're looking for, of course. Coping, mutual support. The way this cheek-by-jowl existence brings out the best in us.

MAM: I wish I could show more grief. I don't want you to think I'm heartless. We were inseparable, only I've got lots to do. Poor Dad. He had everything to live for, basically. I'm sorry I'm not crying. I feel grief-stricken even though I don't show it.

MRS CLEGG: A brave face. They'll understand.

MAM: I do care, deep down.

MRS CLEGG: It'll mean an increased pension.

MAM: Will it?

MRS CLEGG: Plus the death grant.

MAM: Do they give you a death grant?

MRS CLEGG: Provided there's been a death. I put Clifford's towards some loose covers.

MAM: And I suppose I'll still get his disability pension.

MRS CLEGG: What with one thing and another the horizon's far from gloomy.

MAM: He used to have a fine body, right up until his accident. He'd no feeling in this arm.

MRS CLEGG: He's no feeling in it now.

MAM: I suppose we've got to wash him all over.

MRS CLEGG: Of course.

MAM: His eyebrows want cutting.

MRS CLEGG: Never mind his eyebrows. Let's get his trousers off. Do you find this distasteful?

MAM: I'd find it more distasteful if he were alive, bless him! You're such a help, Nora. You should have been a nurse. So calm.

MRS CLEGG: I try to be warm, but clinical. It's a fine line. I'll loosen his trousers.

MAM: I haven't seen some of this for years. (*She weeps.*)

MRS CLEGG: Let it come, love. Let it come.

MAM: I did love him, Nora. I did. I loved him like a child. Only now it's too late.

MRS CLEGG: What's the best way to get his trousers off? You get his legs, and I'll pull.

MAM: Nora.

MRS CLEGG: What?

MAM: Would you be bitterly offended if I took his trousers off by myself?

MRS CLEGG: You can't do it without help.

MAM: I've got to try. He was a shy man, Nora.

MRS CLEGG: Connie. He's not here. He's gone. This is just the shell. The husk. If you're not conscious you can't be self-conscious. I'm thinking of your back.

MAM: You've been so good. So understanding.

MRS CLEGG: I've just been a neighbour, Connie. It's what neighbours are for. Anyway, please yourself. Give us a shout if there's anything you can't manage.

(MS CRAIG *approaches*.)

You don't want her watching if you don't want me.

MAM: But isn't she official? She's got to be here.

(MRS CLEGG *talks quietly to her observer while* MAM *gets on with washing* DAD.)

MRS CLEGG: You'll probably think I'm old-fashioned, Adrian, but my view is that when death occurs in the home, tragic though it is, we should try to think of it as a privilege. So many of the fundamental experiences of our lives have passed beyond our personal control. Passed into the hands of doctors, social workers, nurses and the like so we are denied that contact with birth, sickness and death, with poverty, with suffering and all those areas of human experience...

MAM: Nora! (*Awestruck*)

MRS CLEGG: ... which were the birthright of our parents ...

MAM: Nora! (*Alarm*).

MRS CLEGG: ... and gave their lives meaning and nourishment ...

MAM: NORA!

(MRS CLEGG *goes over*.)

Look.

MRS CLEGG: Good garden rhubarb! What's that? Oh, Connie.

(*They cling to one another, gazing at* MR CRAVEN's *body and at one part in particular*.)

MAM: And you said he was dead.

MRS CLEGG: He may still be dead.

MAM: That's not dead. That's alive. That's life, that is.

MRS CLEGG: It may not be. It may just be a side effect. The muscles contract. The body plays tricks. The dead often seem to grin. This doesn't mean they are happy.

MAM: One touch of the flannel. The sly bugger. And me thinking he was all dead and decent.

MRS CLEGG: Don't leap to conclusions.

MAM: I don't know where to look. And of course we would have company.

MRS CLEGG: Adrian. You'll have been to university. Would you say he was dead?

(ADRIAN *takes a look but says nothing.* MS CRAIG *has gone back to her chair.*)

MAM: I blame you.

MRS CLEGG: Me?

MAM: You would wash him. You would make out that's what it is we do. Traditionally. Normal procedure. For their benefit. Folks don't wash the dead and lay them out. Not in this day and age. It's what my mother used to do. This is the twentieth century. You call in an expert.

MRS CLEGG: She's forgotten. You see how it is. Love, Chippendales has changed hands. It's a patio-paving centre.

MAM: The Co-op hasn't changed hands. That's not a patio-paving centre. The Co-op does a perfectly adequate funeral. I've attended several and they couldn't be faulted. Besides which they'd come along with all this at their fingertips. They'd know if it was normal or not. Tie it down. Tether it. They'll be past masters, with diplomas. They wouldn't turn a hair. But oh no. It had to be Do It Yourself. We're supposed to behave normally.

MRS CLEGG: It's no problem for you. You can behave normally. You forget they're there half the time and when you remember you don't know what it is they're there for.

MAM: Well what are they there for? I don't know.

MRS CLEGG: What difference does it make. It's an unlooked for situation, this. Stuck in a room with a corpse that's not fit to be seen. I know one thing. If it were in my house I could rise to it magnificently.

MAM: You keep saying corpse. Corpse. We don't know if he is a corpse. I've only got your word for it. And all the evidence points the other way. The blighter. It's the same as when he was alive. Always trying to spring it on you. And don't keep looking at him. That's my husband. Saying you bake. You never bake. She never bakes. It's all bought stuff in her house.

55

It always has been. You were always running on to the end, you, when there was an end to run on to. That's what killed your Clifford. Chips and bought cakes. What do you do for your dinner now they've pulled down the chip shop?

MRS CLEGG: She's under stress. Only you see what I have to put up with. I don't think we can do any more good here, Adrian. I'll see if I can find you a few home-made scones and some of my own preserves. And perhaps when he's made up his mind whether he's coming or going I'll bob in again. It's no joke being a tower of strength round here, I can tell you.

(MRS CLEGG *and* ADRIAN *leave.* MAM *and* MS CRAIG *are alone.*)

MAM: Give me that towel. I said give me that towel.

(MS CRAIG *does so.*)

Thank you. Now. I'm not leaving him stuck here. We'd better get him back in the chair. Come on. Frame.

(MAM *and* MS CRAIG *move him on to the chair.*)

Watching. Not feeling. And what if anybody comes? This is what children are designed for, this. Buckling to. Rallying round. And where are they? One's marrying a blackie and I don't know where the other is. Our Terry. I loved him. He can't have loved me, I've never had a postcard. I had a record played for him on Family Favourites on the off-chance he was in Australia. There's a limit to what you can do.

I had visions of him going to university. I can just see him in a scarf opening a bank account.

He's married probably now. Kiddies. I could be stood here and all the time I'm a grandmother with cartloads of snaps to catch up on. Instead of which I'm alone. Nobody to turn to. No kids. Nobody. (*'I Can Give You the Starlight'* (*Novello,* The Dancing Years) *begins quietly and it seems as if* MS CRAIG *is about to speak when there is a bang on the door.*) Oh, company!

(*She opens the door and* LINDA *comes in, lugging two suitcases, exhausted.*)

(*Brightly*) Hello, Linda love. Have you come back?

LINDA: No. This is a mirage. I'm at this moment sitting under a palm tree in one of the OPEC countries. (*She goes to the*

door which she has left open.) Come in if you're coming.
(*There is a pause and a large man* (SID) *in working clothes
enters.*)

MAM: Hello. Are you another one? They seem to be doing a
very thorough job. Sit down. Make yourself at home.

SID: Thank you.

MAM: Oh, quite talkative. What happend to your fiancé, love?
Did you not hit it off?

LINDA: I never saw him.

MAM: You were all set to marry him.

LINDA: Well I didn't, did I?
(*Pause*)
Though I got shortlisted.

MAM: Shortlisted? For his bride? How many of you were there?

LINDA: Twenty-five.

MAM: Twenty-five prospective brides? What sort of a man is that?

LINDA: It wasn't him. He wasn't even there. He'd had to fly off
to Vienna. It was his agent, somebody from Lloyds Bank.

MAM: Lloyds? That's one of the classier banks. I'd go there if I
had any money.

LINDA: I got as far as the last six then got eliminated.

MAM: What did you fall down on? Your shorthand?

LINDA: No! My tits!

MAM: Don't be bitter. I'm sure that's not the kind of thing he
was looking for, not if he was from Lloyds Bank.

LINDA: Listen, we had to parade up and down the Wharfedale
Room in our bra and panties!

MAM: At the Queen's Hotel? And it's where Sir Malcolm
Sargent used to stay!

LINDA: He said that although I'd done very well in the oral
examination my tits fell short of the standard required.

MAM: Fell short?

LINDA: He said they were small and a bit on the old side.

MAM: The cheek.

LINDA: What do they know about tits at Lloyds Bank?

MAM: Quite. Still I'm glad you've come back because we've had
a bit of bad news about your father.

LINDA: I thought he was quiet. Is he dead?

57

MAM: Possibly. It's not completely clear. There's evidence on both sides. I'd welcome your opinion.

(LINDA *lifts the towel covering* DAD.)

LINDA: Blood and sand!

MAM: Exactly.

LINDA: I don't know much about death. Is that what it looks like?

MAM: Yes and no.

LINDA: If he's dead what's he doing in the house?

MAM: Nowadays it is unusual. It was much more the thing when we were younger.

LINDA: Get him out of here. This is the twentieth century.

MAM: Linda, he's your father.

LINDA: Yes. I want to show some feeling and get him into the fridge. I can't understand. You were always so houseproud. What's Sid going to think.

SID: Don't mind me. I've got a family of my own.

MAM: This is a departure: gab, gab, gab.

LINDA: Have you notified the authorities?

MAM: I don't think so. I can't remember.

LINDA: Why not?

MAM: I'm beat, Linda. I'm weary. I'm just at the far end.

LINDA: You can't leave him stuck there. Notify somebody.

MAM: I will once I've got him washed.

LINDA: No. Now. Write it down so you don't forget. (*She does so.*) Dad dead. Burial required.

MAM: Why can't you do it?

LINDA: You're his wife.

MAM: We reckon to be a family.

LINDA: Family nothing. All you need do is tell them and they'll be round to fetch him like a shot. It's bread and butter to somebody is that. Stuck there. Life is for living, that's my motto.

MAM: I'll get me washed and go up to the Co-op.

LINDA: Why can't she go?

MAM: It's not her place. Why can't he go?

LINDA: What's it to do with him?

SID: My wife's in a steel collar. She had one of these accidents in

58

the home. The home is more dangerous than the roads apparently. In terms of statistics.

MAM: That's fascinating. I wish she'd take a leaf out of your book.

LINDA: You'd better come upstairs.

MAM: Yes. Go upstairs. Have a meander round. Show him your room, love. Your home environment. All part of the picture.

LINDA: (*Wearily*) Mam.

MAM: And Linda.

(LINDA *pauses.*)

Don't be upset about Saudi Arabia. Plenty more fish in the sea.

(LINDA *and* SID *go upstairs.*)

She's a resilient girl. She'll soon bounce back. (*Pause*) Only I shall have it all to do, I can see that. The death and all the donkey work. He'd have taken all this in his stride. But then he'd been educated.

(*Music starts.*)

Did I tell you I had a son?

Terry his name was.

He loved music. Adored music. Dad was tone deaf. I had perfect pitch. So where are you? I could have been in the Philharmonic Chorus, you know.

Asked round to these coffee parties after rehearsals, cocktails, little savoury things. There's no telling where I could have ended. Another Kathleen Ferrier possibly. She had a northern background. It didn't stop her.

(*During this last speech* MAM *and* MS CRAIG *have begun to dance and* MAM *sings 'I Can Give You the Starlight', the music swelling under her singing as they dance.*)

You're light as a feather.

(*They dance in great style. When they stop they continue to hold one another for a moment.*)

MS CRAIG: Mam.

MAM: About bloody time! Got up in that costume. It doesn't suit you. It doesn't suit you one bit. Navy's your colour. You always looked lovely in navy. Give your Mam a kiss. I think on the whole I preferred you in sportscoat and flannels.

59

MS CRAIG: Those days are over.

MAM: Terry. Are you still Terry?

MS CRAIG: I spell it with an 'i'.

MAM: You didn't have far to go then?

MS CRAIG: My friends call me Kim.

MAM: Kim. That's a nice name. I prefer Kim to Terri. Kim's more classy. I never thought I'd have a son called Kim. Let alone a daughter. You wouldn't recognize Leeds. It's all pedestrianized now. The traffic's been secluded. And one way and another all your Aunties have died. Mrs Metcalf's had a stroke and their David now works in computers in Kettering. Has anything much else happened apart from you changing your name? Are you rich?

MS CRAIG: To some extent.

MAM: That's good. Though money isn't everything. Did you get a degree?

MS CRAIG: Yes. At Cambridge.

MAM: Cambridge. That's nice. You get all that from me. Your father never opened a book in his life, bless him. (*She goes and looks at him.*) No change. His thing's still there. Shocking except he wasn't all that bad. Considering you were his only son he didn't really dislike you. I shall miss him in other ways. I've missed *you*.

MS CRAIG: I've missed you too.

MAM: Linda hasn't changed, has she?

MS CRAIG: She has a bit.

MAM: She's a personal secretary, you know.

(MS CRAIG *nods.*)

She goes all over. She won't be here long before she's setting off. Stockholm. Kuala Lumpur. If it's not one place it's another. (*Pause*) Actually I don't believe that. Your Dad did. He thought she was a personal secretary. I didn't disillusion him. I don't think she's a personal secretary at all. You don't wear them hairy pink jumper things if you're a personal secretary. No, she lets us think she's a secretary but do you know what I think she is? A policewoman: that would account for her odd hours, bobbing in and out. I wouldn't put it past her to be on detective work. What do

60

you think, Kim?

MS CRAIG: It's possible, Connie.

MAM: That shows you've gone up in the world, using my name. Better-class children do that. Treat their parents like people. Oh, Kim.

MS CRAIG: I'm going to take you away, Connie.

MAM: Where, Kim? London? I've always dreamed about going to London. Most people have made at least one visit by the time they reach my age. Let's have a day or two in London and it will remove the stigma.

MS CRAIG: I'm going to take you away for good! You're going to be protected.

MAM: What from? Not your Dad? He's dead.

MS CRAIG: Everything. Life. You're going to be looked after, Connie. Sheltered. Cared for.

MAM: It's a home, isn't it? You're going to put me in a home. You've come back just to put me in a home. Well, I'm not ready. I'm not silly. My memory's bad but I'm not incontinent. I don't want to go into a home. I want to go into the horrible new flats. Oh, Terry Craven, what a trick to do.

MS CRAIG: It's not a home, Connie. I wouldn't put you in a home.

MAM: Children always say that. That's what I said to my mother. And we did. We did. She lost her memory and we put her in a home.

MS CRAIG: Connie, I promise you. It's not a home. Listen.

MAM: No, you listen. You can't just put me in a home the way I put my mother in a home. It's not as simple as that now. There's people on the Council can stop you. Wardens, social workers. Old people now, they have to be treated with imagination, it's the law. And I'm not old. It's just that I forget. You and me were such pals.

MS CRAIG: Mam, how many more times, I don't mean a home.

MAM: Will you promise me? Promise me over the body of your father you will not put me in a home.

MS CRAIG: I promise you over the body of my father I will not put you in a home.

MAM: (*Pointing*) It's gone. Look, it's gone. Oh, Terry. It must just have been his way of saying goodbye. Oh, Wilf, forgive me, Wilf.

DAD: Wilf? What's this Wilf? What's happened?

MAM: Dad? Are you not dead? We thought you were dead.

DAD: You were wrong then, weren't you? You were premature. What's been the matter with me?

MAM: You passed out.

DAD: What am I like this for? Tied up?

MAM: You're not tied up.

DAD: I'm bound hand and foot.

MAM: You never are.

DAD: I can't move. I'm in water.

MAM: No.

DAD: I'm in water up to my neck.

MAM: You're at home. Look.

DAD: How look? I can't look. I'm in plaster from head to foot. I'm paralysed.

MAM: You weren't paralysed a minute ago. Sit for a bit and it'll go off.

DAD: Sit? I can't move.

MAM: It may be nerves. Nervous paralysis. People go for years thinking they can't move a muscle and it's nothing but their imagination.

DAD: It was that youth. Banging my steel plate, and her just sat there.

MAM: No.

DAD: She sat there and watched.

MAM: You're confused.

DAD: He was banging it up and down like a coal-hole lid while she never lifted a finger.

MAM: She'd never do that. Another human being. We thought you were dead.

DAD: I bet.

MAM: I was just learning to accommodate. You do lead us a dance.

DAD: I can't bloody move. Feel me. See if there's any feeling left.

MAM: I won't. I'm not starting on that game again.

DAD: Light me a cig.

MAM: I won't light you a cig. Light your own cig.

DAD: I can't move.

MAM: Use it as a challenge.

DAD: Our Linda'd light me one. Our Linda'd care.

MAM: Our Linda. Our Linda. You're going to have to change your tune a bit. There's going to have to be less of our Linda now.

(MS CRAIG *lights* MR CRAVEN *a cigarette, putting it in her mouth then his.*)

MS CRAIG: Change your brand, Dad? These give you a more satisfying smoke, do they?

DAD: What do you know about a satisfying smoke. You're not man enough to know about a satisfying smoke. That's how I knew you were a nancy: you never smoked.

MAM: He smokes now, don't you love. Can't criticize him on that score.

DAD: Coming in all dolled up. I knew you straight off.

MAM: I would have done if it hadn't been for my memory.

DAD: Frocks. I caught him in one of your frocks once. While you were out. I was physically sick. My own son. He'd be fifteen then. I thought it was just a phase. I ought to have known. There were other signs. Most lads would have at least one unwanted pregnancy to their credit by the time they got to that age. Not our Terry.

MAM: His name's Kim, now, isn't it, love? I'm very happy for him. Her.

DAD: A bit of beef skirt, that's what he is. He wanted me killed. He looked on while I was assaulted.

MAM: Only as part of his job. He was conscientious even as a boy.

DAD: I can't *move*.

MAM: That's not Kim's fault. She's come to take us away, haven't you, Kim?

MS CRAIG: Yes, Connie.

DAD: *Connie?* Who the fuck's Connie?

MAM: Me, I'm Connie.

DAD: Don't you Connie, her, madam. I'm the one who Connie's her. She's Mam to you. Mam. Dad. Connie.

MAM: I'm Mam to you too. You never say my name.

DAD: I choose my moments. I say it when it's appropriate. Kim. Connie. Have you both gone mad? You dirty sods. You dirty stinking sods. Using your names. You disgust me.

MAM: Dad.

DAD: You wanted me dead. You thought I was dead. 'Wilf'.

MAM: We had begun to bank on it a bit, I must admit, however, let's change the subject. Kim's got a proposition to make.

MS CRAIG: I've come to take you away, Dad.

MAM: Where is it you're taking us, love?

MS CRAIG: It's on the outskirts.

MAM: Does that mean the Green Belt? It's been one of Dad's ambitions to live on the outskirts.

MS CRAIG: It's in a park.

MAM: I never dreamed I would end up in a park.

DAD: What sort of park? Homes are in parks. The outskirts are where all the homes are. He's going to put us in a home. Your son, stroke daughter.

MAM: It's not a home. Terry has promised me faithfully it's not a home.

DAD: You told your mother it was a hotel. A private hotel.

MAM: No.

DAD: She was just going there for the weekend while we went to Scarborough.

MAM: No.

DAD: She couldn't speak when we saw her next. She'd gone silly.

MAM: No.

DAD: Yes. It's a home.

MAM: God forgive you, Terry. Your own mother.

(GREGORY *opens the door and comes inside, waiting.*
ADRIAN *follows and waits, the other side.*
HARMAN *enters. The same age as* GREGORY *and* ADRIAN, *but with more authority. He is followed by two more young men,* CHARLES *and* ROWLAND, *who wait in the background, holding clipboards.*)

HARMAN: And if there is a problem get on to Maintenance and let them sort it out. It's what we pay them for. Now. What have we here?

(HARMAN *walks round the house and round* MAM *and* DAD

without speaking. GREGORY *and* ADRIAN *follow,* GREGORY *with a notebook,* ADRIAN *with a Polaroid camera.*)

(*After an excessive silence*) The mantelpiece is perfect. Pity they ruined the fireplace.

(GREGORY *makes a note.*)

The curtains are good.

(ADRIAN *snaps the curtains.*)

All this is beautiful.

(HARMAN *maybe frames a section of the room in his hands and* ADRIAN *then photographs it.* HARMAN *opens the staircase door.*) Get a sample of that wallpaper. It's terrible. (*He sees the bath.*) I like the bath. The bath comes over loud and clear. (HARMAN *now looks very closely at* MAM *and* DAD, *without speaking. He maybe runs his hand over* MAM's *face absently.*) Hello, love.

MAM: Hello.

DAD: Who the fuck are you?

HARMAN: Hello! Are you the man of the house?

MAM: My husband's not himself at the moment.

(HARMAN, GREGORY, ADRIAN *and* MS CRAIG *now confer.*)

HARMAN: My feeling is we should take this place. As it stands. In fact don't let's piss around. We should take the whole street.

MS CRAIG: I thought so.

DAD: Who is this joker? Lay off.

(HARMAN *is standing by* DAD, *massaging his arm.*)

HARMAN: You're understandably intrigued, Mr Craven. Your home invaded . . . are you totally paralysed? . . . habits documented by strangers . . . do you feel that? . . . your everyday life subject to scrutiny . . . no? . . . the flesh is so good: white, white, *white.*

(GREGORY *makes a note.*)

DAD: Mam.

MAM: It's all right, Dad. He's from the Council. It's to do with all-round happiness. We had the explanatory letter.

DAD: Happiness nothing, I require medical attention.

HARMAN: When Kim mentioned her family to me, Mrs Craven, I was quite frankly surprised. I never knew you had a family, Kim, I said. I had you down as an independent sort of person. And here you are. A queen. (I love the face, Kim.) We send out expeditions to Brazil. We plunge through the rain forests of the Amazon to protect a few lost tribes. But it's here, Mrs Craven, now. This is the disappearing world. Leeds, Bradford, Halifax. A way of life on its last legs. Women like you . . .

MAM: I'm old-fashioned, I know . . .

HARMAN: This house . . . this street.

MAM: They're grand houses. I've always said so. It's a crime to knock them down.

HARMAN: Absolutely. Show her, Adrian.

(ADRIAN *takes* MAM *to the door.*)

DAD: Slums.

HARMAN: No.

MAM: They've gone. The bulldozers have gone.

DAD: They'll be knocking off early, the buggers.

MAM: (*And possibly she goes outside the house so we just hear her echoing voice*) There isn't a bulldozer to be seen.

HARMAN: No. I had them withdrawn.

DAD: Then unwithdraw them. We're waiting to get into the new flats.

HARMAN: He's such value.

MS CRAIG: I know. I hate him.

HARMAN: Naturally.

MAM: Are we not going to be knocked down then?

HARMAN: Yes, but very lovingly and by qualified experts. Each brick numbered; a chart made for every slate, the whole house, the entire street to be re-erected on the outskirts in a parkland setting.

DAD: It's a home.

MAM: It's not a home, Dad. These are all refined young men.

HARMAN: A park people will pay to go into. A people's park.

MAM: We shan't be with zebras and kangaroos. We went to one of those once and they were all asleep. It was money down the drain.

HARMAN: Visitors will alight from one of a fleet of trams to find themselves in a close-knit community where people know each others' names and still stop and pass the time of day.

There will be a cotton mill, steam engines and genuine hardship.

MAM: This park, is it in a clean-air zone?

HARMAN: Unfortunately yes, but on certain appointed days soot will fall like rain, exactly as it used to.

MAM: But will I be able to keep the place spotless?

HARMAN: Only by working your fingers to the bone.

DAD: Will there be a fireside?

HARMAN: A coal fire is a must, though underfloor central heating is provided strictly for use out of opening hours.

MAM: I like a fire. A fire's company.

DAD: This fire, can I spit into it?

HARMAN: At will and never accurately.

MAM: That means I shall have to blacklead.

HARMAN: Constantly.

MAM: What will I cook?

HARMAN: Tripe, cowheel, trotters, breast of mutton. The traditional food of your class.

MAM: I hope you've got an understanding butcher. And I can bake. Bake like I did when I was first married.

DAD: You never baked. My mother baked. You never did.

MAM: I did, I'm sure I did. Quiches are the in thing now, aren't they? All the young marrieds go in for quiches. I keep reading about it in these magazines. I imagine you have quiches, Kim? You have done well.

MS CRAIG: It'll be exactly like it was when I was little.

MAM: I can't remember what I was like when you were little.

MS CRAIG: Don't worry. I can.

MAM: Was I a good mother? A capable housewife?

MS CRAIG: Down to the last detail.

MAM: I never let you go short?

MS CRAIG: With you self-sacrifice always came first.

MAM: I sound to have been a perfect mother.

MS CRAIG: You were.

HARMAN: And shall be again. And people coming round will watch you work and skimp and save and remember the labour their mothers had and all for nothing and will go away contented and assured of the future. And if you do forget, don't worry; it simply tells another story.

DAD: What's in it for you?

HARMAN: We're a young team. We do it for love.

DAD: Love! I'm paralysed.

MAM: Has it not gone off yet? It will, I'm sure. Try to look on the bright side.

DAD: I don't want to go.

MAM: I do.

HARMAN: Perfect. The woman clings to the past, the man holds out for the future. You were right, Kim. They are ideal.

DAD: I want our Linda.

MAM: It doesn't sound to me in Linda's line. Ask her.

DAD: How can I ask her? She's in Saudi Arabia.

MAM: She's not in Saudi Arabia. She's upstairs.

MS CRAIG: Linda can come if she wants.

DAD: I'm not going anywhere without Linda. Me and Linda are inseparable.

HARMAN: I must go. Dear lady. Put one or two things together, but only the barest essentials. Packing is unnecessary as these trained staff will shortly transfer your home and its contents to its new setting. Nothing will change.

MAM: That's ideal.

HARMAN: The only difference, unavoidable in the circumstances, is that your windows will have a distant prospect of green fields. That apart, no expense has been spared to convince you that you are still living in the depths of the slums.

MAM: It sounds a work of art. I'm so excited. I've always felt the past was over and that I'd somehow missed it. Now it's starting all over again.

(HARMAN *kisses* MAM *on both cheeks*.)

That's the classy way of kissing, isn't it? Do you kiss like that, Kim? Oh, love, I'm so proud! (*She goes upstairs.*)

DAD: I'm not coming. I refuse to move.

HARMAN: Warm. Familiar. A genuine community where misfortune brings not isolation but a spate of visitors. Neighbours (with broth, possibly). A family doctor, your name at his fingertips, a vicar of stout faith to whom consolation is second nature. A place, Dad. *Roots. Home.* It's such a powerful image I'm loath to lose him.

MS CRAIG: He embarrasses me.

HARMAN: Of course.

DAD: Young man. Young man, I've something to tell you, something that will change your ideas. That's not a woman. I'm ashamed to say that's my son. He's a lad dressed up. Or something.

HARMAN: (*Whispering*) I *know*. (*He goes back to* MS CRAIG *and the others.*) We must have him.

DAD: I shall write personally to the Town Hall.

HARMAN: Bless you. Kim's a big feather in their cap. We're very proud of Kim, aren't we?

DAD: I feel sick.

(HARMAN *kisses* MS CRAIG.)

HARMAN: Do your best. (*To* DAD.) Goodbye. And don't change. (HARMAN *goes.* GREGORY, ADRIAN, ROWLAND *and* CHARLES *remain.*)

MS CRAIG *looks at the magazine that has the pictures of* LINDA *in it.*)

DAD: That's mine. Put it away. Don't let her see it.

(MS CRAIG *goes on looking at it.*)

You'd never get into a magazine like that. *Kim.* Magazines like that . . . they go into thousands of homes. They're distributed in every part of the English-speaking world. She's famous is our Linda. She's a known face. She'll get correspondence from all over. Be asked to open precincts, supermarkets, betting-shops. You can't despise fame.

(MS CRAIG *puts the magazine away.* LINDA *comes in.*)

That's your brother, Linda.

LINDA: I had a feeling it might be. Hi. Long time no see.

DAD: Doesn't he disgust you?

LINDA: Should he?

DAD: He disgusts me.

LINDA: I find him not unattractive.

DAD: It's unnatural.

LINDA: Dad. This is the twentieth century. Mam was telling me about the museum. I won't come if it's all the same to you. Quite frankly I don't feel part of this environment any more.

(LINDA *and* MS CRAIG *are smiling at one another*.)
We've both of us had to break out. In our different ways.

DAD: Don't bracket yourself with him, Linda. You're a personal secretary. He's bent.

LINDA: I knew that years ago. I knew it as soon as I saw the photographs in his room.

DAD: Male nudes?

LINDA: Judy Garland.

DAD: Don't leave me, Linda. I don't fancy being in a glass case. I want my declining years to be spent with you.

LINDA: Be practical. You can't be with me.

DAD: Why?

LINDA: I work late; I often bring work home.

DAD: I find the sound of typing soothing.

LINDA: Typing! (*She laughs.*) Sid was telling me upstairs he has a brother-in-law with a string of launderettes all over the Channel Islands. He thinks I may be qualified for an executive post.

DAD: Could there be a position for me?

LINDA: Dad, you're paralysed from the neck downwards.

DAD: It sounds a large organization, there might just be a niche.

LINDA: Oh Dad.

DAD: I blame you. She'd have stayed if it hadn't been for you. What did you want to come back for?

MS CRAIG: I wanted to refresh my memory. It's my job.

DAD: Your job to stir things up. Your job to provoke. Your job to sit there, casting an educated eye. We were a more or less united family on the threshold of a nice modern flat. Now Linda's leaving and your Mam and me are stuck in a museum the rest of our lives. Stay the same? It's a revolution.

MS CRAIG: Some degree of interference in the social processes is inevitable. The trained observer makes allowances for that. (MS CRAIG *gives* LINDA *the magazine*.)

DAD: No. Don't look, Linda. Take no notice. You, you're a passive observer. You're not supposed to take a hand.

MS CRAIG: I'm your son, Dad.

DAD: You want me killed.

LINDA: (*To* MS CRAIG) Is this yours?

70

MS CRAIG: No. It's our Dad's.

LINDA: But you thought I was a personal secretary.

DAD: Not altogether.

LINDA: You thought I was a typist.

DAD: I always had an inkling.

LINDA: You never let on?

DAD: Out of love, Linda. Out of consideration. Out of tact.

LINDA: Your only daughter drifts into prostitution and you don't lift a finger.

DAD: It's not prostitution, Linda. It's art. Fame. Those magazines go all over. People will know you who've never seen you. In Denmark or West Germany! I just wanted you to get on.

LINDA: You disgust me.

DAD: We were always such pals.

LINDA: He interfered with me, that's what he means.
(*She shows* MS CRAIG *the magazine.*)
Nice wallpaper, don't you think. To look at him you'd never dream he'd got a degree in philosophy would you. Some daughters would have reported you. You could be had up. Sent to prison.

DAD: Don't say such things. You're hurting me.

LINDA: They gave me that candlestick. It's upstairs.

DAD: I've still got feelings.

LINDA: I was supposed to be the apple of your eye. That's one of them continental quilts. She's from Birmingham. You can tell as soon as she opens her mouth.

DAD: I love you, Linda.

LINDA: Too late. I'm not a personal secretary. I'm a slag.

DAD: We could still be together. I could be standing by.

LINDA: Do you mean watching?

DAD: Some people like being watched. Being watched improves it for some people. Alters it. Makes it different.

LINDA: You can hardly see.

DAD: They won't know that. You've got to adapt to changing circumstances. I've been slow to adapt. Looking back I can see that's been my problem all the way through. Come on, Linda. We could make an enterprising duo and we'd be together.

71

LINDA: Dad!

DAD: I've still a bit of a future left. If you leave me I shall be on my own.

LINDA: You won't. You'll be in the park with Mam. There'll be people traipsing round every day, looking at you. They'll be watching you all the time. You won't be lonely. You'll never have a moment to yourself. And there'll always be Kim to pop in and keep an eye on you. I'm telling you, you'll be in clover. Bye-bye, chick.

(LINDA *kisses* DAD *on the top of his head.* MAM *comes in looking very smart.*)

MAM: Are you off, love? Where is it this time? Winnipeg? Santa Fé?

LINDA: Actually I'm just popping across to Jersey.

DAD: Jersey! Show her. Show your Mam that magazine. Go on. See whether that's Jersey. Look. That's not Jersey. It's filth.

(MAM *looks at the magazine.*)

MAM: Well, times change. You've got to keep up with the times.

DAD: It's our Linda.

MAM: Top secretaries, they do get their pictures in magazines.

DAD: She's no clothes on.

MAM: They use nudes to sell office furniture now. It's the modern world. Bye-bye, love. Spare us a thought when you're coming through the duty free. Say goodbye to Kim.

DAD: Don't let him touch you, Linda. He may be successful, but he's still a nancy.

LINDA: He obviously fancies me. How can he be a nancy?

DAD: He's wearing a frock so it's still wrong.

MAM: It's clear you could have had a lovely brother-and-sister relationship. What a pity you're going now we're all together.

LINDA: (*Shouts upstairs*) Sid.

DAD: Kiss me, Linda. Just give me a kiss.

MAM: Now Dad, don't spoil it.

(SID *appears.*)

LINDA: I hope these launderettes aren't a figment of your imagination.

SID: Thank you for letting me see your lovely home.

72

MAM: It's been a pleasure. Off you go.
   (SID and LINDA depart.)
DAD: Linda!
   (MAM stands, a bit lost.)
MAM: Now, I'm all dressed up and I know we're going somewhere but I've forgotten where it is. Are we going to London, Kim?
DAD: She's getting worse. You don't know what you're taking on. She'll drive you mad. We're going into cold storage, you dozy cow. We're headed for a glass case.
MAM: We're not going into a home?
MS CRAIG: No, Mam. It's not a home.
DAD: It's worse than a home.
MAM: It can't be. There's nowhere worse than a home. My mother went into a home. I've never forgiven myself.
DAD: Now it's our turn.
MS CRAIG: Listen, it's your life as it used to be, down to the last detail. But it's not a home. It's this home, for ever and ever. I promise.
   (At this point GREGORY, ADRIAN, ROWLAND and CHARLES begin to dismantle the house. Large sections of the room are removed, walls, furniture, the lot.)
MAM: If Kim says it isn't a home, Dad, I think we should believe her. So let's get you dressed and ready. She's been educated and (MAM watches as a wall is silently and smoothly removed.) they seem to know exactly what they're doing.
DAD: He tried to kill me.
MAM: When? With the car? She probably doesn't even drive. Oh, Dad.
DAD: What's matter?
MAM: You're all wet. Why didn't you say you wanted to go?
DAD: I didn't know. I've told you, I can't feel anything.
MAM: I've just put my best frock on.
DAD: It's not my fault.
MAM: Where's your clean pants?
   (MAM manages to rescue a pair from a piece of furniture which is on one of the sections being removed. She does this as if it is the most natural thing in the world.)

This puts a different complexion on things. If he's going to be like this, Kim, he'll want tip-top nursing. I'm not sure I'm up to that.

DAD: You are, Mam, you are.

MAM: In the absence of any labour-saving devices I shall have quite enough to do without you wetting all up and down.

MS CRAIG: We're basically a museum. We haven't the facilities to cope with incontinence.

MAM: Whereas a hospital would have all that at their fingertips. What do you think?

MS CRAIG: You must decide. It must be your decision.

MAM: You are a comfort. I've never had such support from your father.

MS CRAIG: Maybe when we've got you settled in we could look round for somebody else. A nice lodger, perhaps. That's a traditional situation, ideal for a model community.

MAM: He'd have to be clean. A widower perhaps. Someone retired. Gents' outfitters have always seemed to me a nice class of person.

DAD: What are you whispering about? I want to go with you. I want to be preserved too.

MAM: Say if he didn't go, we could advertise for some sort of attendant. A young person wanting to pull their weight in society might just jump at a genuine invalid.

MS CRAIG: That's true.

MAM: Opportunities calling for devoted self-sacrifice don't turn up every day of the week.

MS CRAIG: Quite. Any really first-rate chance of improving the soul gets snapped up by the social services department. (MAM *has been stood with a bowl and towel and now just manages to park them on the next piece of the room that is on its way out.*)

MAM: Another thing, Dad, is now that Kim's come back, Terry as was, I can see how little you and me have got in common. Even memories. Husband and wife you'd think we'd have the same memories, but we don't. My memory's bad, I know that. I take after my mother, but the memories I do have I share with Kim. And she's interested. You're not.

74

You've never been bothered about the past at all. You couldn't wait to get to the future.

DAD: I only want to get into the flat. All this'll be different when we get into the flat.

MAM: No, love. You'll be better off in the new wing at the Infirmary. It's the last word in architecture as well as treatment. It was opened by the Duchess of Kent.

DAD: I won't wet myself again, I promise.

MAM: It doesn't matter if you do, love. It'll all be catered for by the nurses, it's part of their training. We'll be able to bob in and see you any time: they're very liberal about visiting hours now. It's this new dispensation: you can pop in any time provided you don't actually see the patients being treated. (*She goes out, calling.*) Don't take away the scullery till I've washed my hands.

(*The scullery is removed.* DAD *and* MS CRAIG *are now left on a completely open stage.*)

DAD: Don't leave me, Terry. You've been educated, you can't abandon me. I love you. I know I loved Linda more but you can't always love your children fifty-fifty.

MS CRAIG: Don't worry about it, Dad.

DAD: Take me with you. I'll even use your name. I'd call you . . . Kim.

MS CRAIG: You wouldn't enjoy it.

DAD: I would. I'd enjoy anywhere. I enjoy life. I just need the right circumstances. Given the proper environment I'd be a different person.

MS CRAIG: No.

DAD: Then kill me. Don't leave me. Kill me.

MS CRAIG: I don't want to kill you.

DAD: You always wanted to kill me. So go on. Get it over with. (*In the scullery* MAM *starts singing 'We'll Gather Lilacs'* (*Novello,* Perchance to Dream).)

MS CRAIG: No.

DAD: What are you doing?

MS CRAIG: I'm going to kiss you.

DAD: I'd rather you killed me than kissed me. I don't want kissing. Men don't kiss.

75

MS CRAIG: I'm not a man.

DAD: Get away.

MS CRAIG: Go on, Dad. Just a hug.

(*He takes* DAD *and holds* DAD's *face against his chest as* DAD *struggles briefly, then stops.*

MAM *comes back.*)

MAM: Where is it we're bound for? Are we off to London?

MS CRAIG: *No.* The park. Your old life. Remember.

MAM: I don't, love, but you can explain as we go. (*Pause*) You know you remind me of somebody and I've forgotten who it is.

MS CRAIG: Terry, Mam.

MAM: It *is* Terry. I *am* sorry. I shan't forget like this love, once I get settled. There's courses you can take to improve your memory, you see them advertised. I'm going to send up. Your Dad's asleep. Never mind. I knew he wouldn't be interested. Anything that bit unusual you could never get him interested, bless him. I could have had a promising singing career but for him, and he'd never have let you stop on at school. That was all me. I was the one. You get it all from me.

(GREGORY, *having worn a brown coat for the removals, now enters in a white one with a wheelchair.*)

What a spanking wheelchair. Light as a feather. Bye-bye, Wilf. (*Kisses* DAD.) Oh, I've lipsticked you. (*She takes out a hanky and wipes it off.*) We've never really got on. You could tell by our names. Connie and Wilf . . . it doesn't sound right somehow. Not to me anyway. Peggy and Frank, Madge and Perce, Duggie and Maureen . . . they all sound like couples. But Connie and Wilf—that never sounded like anybody to me.

(DAD *is wheeled off by* GREGORY.)

He'll be better off in hospital. Waited on hand and foot.

MS CRAIG: Naturally.

MAM: They're very good that way now. It's wonderful what they do for you. We never had services like that when we were young.

(ADRIAN *takes her arm to the music of 'Did You Not Hear My*

76

Lady' (*Handel*) *sung by* MAM *on tape.*)
Oh, are you my escort? This takes me back to when I was first married. I don't know where we're going but I'm looking forward to it.

I forget everything but never songs. What does that mean?
(MAM *continues singing as she is escorted away, leaving* MS CRAIG *alone.*)

MS CRAIG: That's a load off my mind, seeing them both settled . . . my father didn't die: he'd just swooned from distaste at that physical contact with his ex-son. I shan't stay around long. I've got my sights set on New York. You can be yourself there and nobody turns a hair. Meanwhile I seem to be coming round to my Dad. When I go to see him they wheel him out on to the balcony and we talk. We talk a lot now.

(DAD *and* MAM *appear on either side of the stage,* DAD *in a wheelchair. All three characters remain isolated.*)

DAD: They showed this view to Princess Alexandra when she came round and she said 'This view is as good as any medicine.' You can see the whole of Leeds. I wish I'd branched out a bit now, Terry. I should have been more like you. Do you still wear that stuff?

MS CRAIG: Sometimes.

DAD: You want to blame your Mam.

MAM: I have a young woman comes to see me. I think she must be a social worker. She's quite pleasant but then, that's what she's paid for. She gets cross if I say it's a home. But if it's not a home, what is it?

MS CRAIG: Home for me at the moment is a little place on the edge of the moors, a farmhouse I've done up. It's only forty minutes but it's another world. I look down on everything. Leeds . . . it's just a glow in the sky. I feel I'm ready to start now.